McGRAW-HILL
SCIENCE

Macmillan/McGraw-Hill Edition

Richard Moyer • Lucy Daniel • Jay Hackett
H. Prentice Baptiste • Pamela Stryker • JoAnne Vasquez

NATIONAL
GEOGRAPHIC
SOCIETY

On the Cover:
Gouldian finches are some of the most vividly colorful birds on Earth. There are three varieties—the red-headed, black-headed, and yellow-headed. Their native habitat is the northern region of Australia. They are not as abundant today as they once were, due to loss of habitat.

Mc Graw Hill **Macmillan McGraw-Hill**

New York   Farmington

Program Authors

Dr. Lucy H. Daniel
Teacher, Consultant
Rutherford County Schools, North Carolina

Dr. Jay Hackett
Professor Emeritus of Earth Sciences
University of Northern Colorado

Dr. Richard H. Moyer
Professor of Science Education
University of Michigan-Dearborn

Dr. H. Prentice Baptiste
Professor of Science and Multicultural Education
New Mexico State University
Las Cruces, New Mexico

Pamela Stryker, M.Ed.
Elementary Educator and Science Consultant
Eanes Independent School District
Austin, Texas

Dr. JoAnne Vasquez
Elementary Science Education Consultant
Mesa Public Schools, Arizona
NSTA Past President

learning through listening

Students with print disabilities may be eligible to obtain an accessible, audio version of the pupil edition of this textbook. Please call Recording for the Blind & Dyslexic at 1-800-221-4792 for complete information.

NATIONAL
GEOGRAPHIC
SOCIETY

Washington, D.C.

The features in this textbook entitled "Invitation to Science," "Amazing Stories," and "People in Science," as well as the unit openers, were developed in collaboration with the National Geographic Society's School Publishing Division.

Copyright © 2002 National Geographic Society. All rights reserved.

The name "National Geographic" and the Yellow Border are registered trademarks of the National Geographic Society.

Macmillan/McGraw-Hill

A Division of The McGraw·Hill Companies

ISBN 0-02-280055-7 / 3

1 2 3 4 5 6 7 8 9 058 07 06 05 04 03 02

Consultants

Dr. Carol Baskin
University of Kentucky
Lexington, KY

Dr. Joe W. Crim
University of Georgia
Athens, GA

Dr. Marie DiBerardino
Allegheny University of
Health Sciences
Philadelphia, PA

Dr. R. E. Duhrkopf
Baylor University
Waco, TX

Dr. Dennis L. Nelson
Montana State University
Bozeman, MT

Dr. Fred Sack
Ohio State University
Columbus, OH

Dr. Martin VanDyke
Denver, CO

Dr. E. Peter Volpe
Mercer University
Macon, GA

Consultants

Dr. Clarke Alexander
Skidaway Institute of
Oceanography
Savannah, GA

Dr. Suellen Cabe
Pembroke State University
Pembroke, NC

Dr. Thomas A. Davies
Texas A & M University
College Station, TX

Dr. Ed Geary
Geological Society of America
Boulder, CO

Dr. David C. Kopaska-Merkel
Geological Survey of Alabama
Tuscaloosa, AL

Consultants

Dr. Bonnie Buratti
Jet Propulsion Lab
Pasadena, CA

Dr. Shawn Carlson
Society of Amateur Scientists
San Diego, CA

Dr. Karen Kwitter
Williams College
Williamstown, MA

Dr. Steven Souza
Williamstown, MA

Dr. Joseph P. Straley
University of Kentucky
Lexington, KY

Dr. Thomas Troland
University of Kentucky
Lexington, KY

Dr. Josephine Davis Wallace
University of North Carolina
Charlotte, NC

Consultant for Primary Grades

Donna Harrell Lubcker
East Texas Baptist University
Marshall, TX

Teacher Panelists

Newark, NJ
First Avenue School
Jorge Alameda
Concetta Cioci
Neva Galasso
Bernadette Kazanjian-reviewer
Toby Marks
Janet Mayer-reviewer
Maria Tutela

Brooklyn, NY
P.S. 31
  Janet Mantel
  Paige McGlone
  Madeline Pappas
  Maria Puma-reviewer
P.S. 217
  Rosemary Ahern
  Charles Brown
  Claudia Deeb-reviewer
  Wendy Lerner
P.S. 225
  Christine Calafiore
  Annette Fisher-reviewer

P.S. 250
  Melissa Kane
P.S. 277
  Erica Cohen
  Helena Conti
  Anne Marie Corrado
  Deborah Scott-DiClemente
  Jeanne Fish
  Diane Fromhartz
  Tricia Hinz
  Lisa Iside
  Susan Malament
  Joyce Menkes-reviewer
  Elaine Noto
  Jean Pennacchio
Jeffrey Hampton
Mwaka Yavana

Elmont, NY
Covert Avenue School
Arlene Connelly

Mt. Vernon, NY
Holmes School
Jennifer Cavallaro
Lou Ciofi
George DiFiore
Brenda Durante
Jennifer Hawkins-reviewer
Michelle Mazzotta
Catherine Moringiello
Mary Jane Oria-reviewer
Lucille Pierotti
Pia Vicario-reviewer

Ozone Park, NY
St. Elizabeth School
Joanne Cocchiola-reviewer
Helen DiPietra-reviewer
Barbara Kingston
Madeline Visco

St. Albans, NY
Orvia Williams

UNIT E

Physical Science

Forces and Motion PAGE E1

CHAPTER 9 How Things Move — E2

Lesson 1 Motion and Speed E4

Lesson 2 Forces E12

    Process Skill Builder: Interpret Data E18

    National Geographic Science Magazine:
    Show Your Muscles E20

Lesson 3 Changes in Motion E22

    National Geographic Amazing Stories:
    Speedy Skins E30

Chapter Review E32

CHAPTER 10 Work and Machines — E34

Lesson 4 Doing Work E36

Lesson 5 Levers and Pulleys E42

    National Geographic Science Magazine:
    Simple Machines on a Playground E50

Lesson 6 More Simple Machines E52

    Process Skill Builder: Use Numbers E58

Chapter Review E60

    National Geographic People in Science/Careers E62

Unit Performance Assessment E64

As you study science, you will learn many new words.
You will read about many new ideas. Read these pages.
They will help you understand this book.

1. The **Vocabulary** list has all the new words you will learn in the lesson. The page numbers tell you where the words are taught.

2. The name tells you what the lesson is about.

3. Get Ready uses the picture on the page to help you start thinking about the lesson.

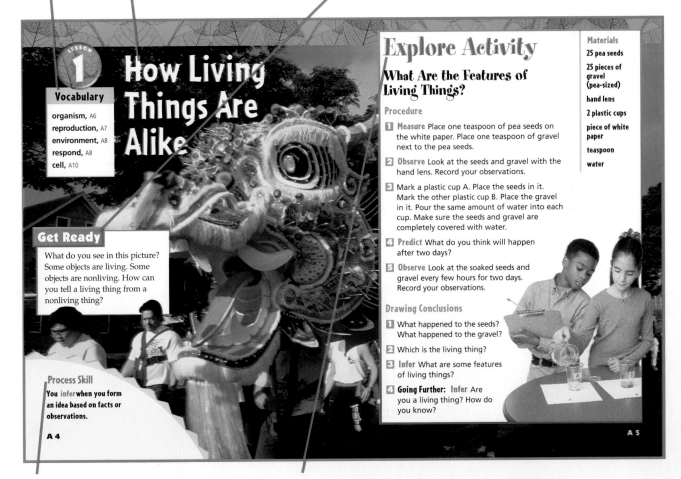

LESSON 1

How Living Things Are Alike

Vocabulary

organism, A6
reproduction, A7
environment, A8
respond, A8
cell, A10

Get Ready

What do you see in this picture? Some objects are living. Some objects are nonliving. How can you tell a living thing from a nonliving thing?

Process Skill

You infer when you form an idea based on facts or observations.

A 4

Explore Activity

What Are the Features of Living Things?

Procedure

1. **Measure** Place one teaspoon of pea seeds on the white paper. Place one teaspoon of gravel next to the pea seeds.

2. **Observe** Look at the seeds and gravel with the hand lens. Record your observations.

3. Mark a plastic cup A. Place the seeds in it. Mark the other plastic cup B. Place the gravel in it. Pour the same amount of water into each cup. Make sure the seeds and gravel are completely covered with water.

4. **Predict** What do you think will happen after two days?

5. **Observe** Look at the soaked seeds and gravel every few hours for two days. Record your observations.

Drawing Conclusions

1. What happened to the seeds? What happened to the gravel?

2. Which is the living thing?

3. **Infer** What are some features of living things?

4. **Going Further: Infer** Are you a living thing? How do you know?

Materials

25 pea seeds

25 pieces of gravel (pea-sized)

hand lens

2 plastic cups

piece of white paper

teaspoon

water

A 5

4. This Process Skill is used in the Explore Activity.

5. The Explore Activity is a hands-on way to learn about the lesson .

As you read a lesson, follow these three steps. They will help you to understand what you are reading.

1. This box contains the **Main Idea** of the lesson. Keep the main idea of the lesson in mind as you read.

2. Before Reading Read the large red question before you read the page. Try to answer this question from what you already know.

3. During Reading Look for new **Vocabulary** words in yellow. Look at the pictures. They will help you understand what you are reading.

Read to Learn

Main Idea All living things have common features.

What Are the Features of Living Things?

An **organism** (AWR·guh·niz·uhm) is a living thing. How can you tell an organism from a nonliving thing? There are certain ways to tell a living thing from a nonliving thing.

Living Things Grow and Change

A living thing grows. It starts out small. Then it gets bigger. An oak tree begins as an acorn. Then it grows to become a green *sapling* (SAP·ling). This is a very young tree.

Organisms also change as they grow. The way a living thing changes during its life is called *development* (di·VEL·uhp·muhnt). As an oak sapling grows, the branches and trunk become thicker and stronger. The oak tree also changes its shape and color as it develops.

Acorn

Large tree

Green sapling

READING Diagrams

How does an oak tree develop?

Young tree

A 6

None of these puppies is an exact copy of its parents. Each puppy has a mixture of features from both parents.

Living Things Reproduce

Another feature of living things is that they make more of their own kind. Plants grow from seeds. Chicks hatch from eggs. Some animals, such as puppies, are born live from their mother. All these are examples of **reproduction** (ree·pruh·DUK·shuhn). This is the way organisms make more of their own kind.

How is a puppy similar to its parents? Some new living things, or offspring, are not exact copies of their parents. Instead, they have characteristics of both parents. Most animal offspring, including you, are not exact copies of their parents.

▶ **What are two features of all living things?** All living things grow and make more of their own kind.

The offspring of a yellow tulip and a red tulip is an orange tulip.

Red tulip

Yellow tulip

Orange tulip

A 7

4. After Reading ▷ This arrow points to a question. It will help you check that you understand what you have read. Try to answer the question before you go to the next large red question.

Physical Science

UNIT E
Forces and Motion

NATIONAL GEOGRAPHIC

NATIONAL GEOGRAPHIC

LOOK!

The wind moves a windmill's blades around and around. Why were these windmills built at different heights?

Forces and Motion

CHAPTER 9

How Things Move E2

CHAPTER 10

Work and Machines E34

CHAPTER

LESSON 1

Motion and
Speed, E4

LESSON 2

Forces, E12

LESSON 3

Changes in
Motion, E22

How Things Move

Did You Ever Wonder?

How fast can a bobsled travel? The chart below
shows that a bobsled travels faster than a speeding
cheetah. It travels even faster than a car on a
highway! What causes objects to move?

Speeds of Objects	Bobsled	Car on Highway	Cheetah
Kilometers per hour	150	105	97
Miles per hour	93	65	60

Motion and Speed

Vocabulary

position, E6
distance, E7
motion, E8
speed, E9

Get Ready

Have you ever been to a pond? Many animals live there. Each animal moves in a different way. A snake slithers along the ground. Fish swim in the water, while turtles crawl on shore. Frogs hop on lily pads, and birds fly overhead. Do you think this lizard moves faster than a fish? How do you know?

Process Skill

You **predict** when you state the possible results of an experiment.

Explore Activity

How Fast Do You Move?

Materials
stopwatch
red crayon
blue crayon
graph paper
meter tape

Procedure

1 **Measure** Measure and mark 10 meters on the floor using the meter tape.

2 **Predict** Predict and record how long you think it will take each group member to walk 10 meters and to run 10 meters.

3 **Measure** Have each person walk 10 meters. Use the stopwatch to measure each person's time. Record each time.

4 Have each person run 10 meters. Measure and record each person's time.

Drawing Conclusions

1 Make a bar graph like the one shown. Use the blue crayon to show walking time. Use the red crayon to show running time. Make a key, and name your graph.

2 What is the difference, in seconds, between your times for walking and running?

3 **Interpret Data** Are the results in the graph similar to your predictions?

4 **Going Further: Predict** How long would it take you to walk 20 meters?

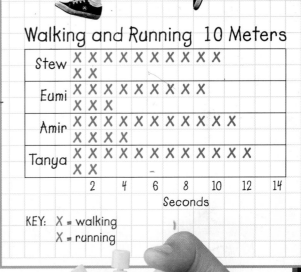

Walking and Running 10 Meters

Stew	X X X X X X X X X X						
Eumi	X X X X X X X X X X X						
Amir	X X X X X X X X X X X X						
Tanya	X X X X X X X X X X X X X X						
	2	4	6	8	10	12	14

Seconds

KEY: X = walking
      X = running

Main Idea You can find out about speed.

How Do You Know If Something Has Moved?

Look at the two pictures of the snail. What has happened? How do you know that the snail has moved?

You know that something has moved because you can see that it has changed **position** (puh·ZISH·uhn). Position is the location of an object. The snail started out at one end of the leaf. It stopped at the other end of the leaf. It changed position.

You can describe an object's position by comparing it with the positions of other objects. Words like *above* and *below, left* and *right, ahead* and *behind* give you clues about position.

Look at the pitcher's mitt in the pictures below. How has its position changed?

Before

After

Before

After

E 6

You can use a ruler to measure distance.

You can measure how far things move. **Distance** (DIS·tuhns) is the length between two places. When an object moves, it goes from a starting position to an ending position. Measuring the length between the starting and ending positions gives you distance. Knowing the distance tells you how far the object has moved.

Comparing How Far Objects Move

1. Place one ruler on the floor to mark a starting line.

2. **Experiment** Set a crumpled piece of paper on the floor in front of the ruler. Blow it across the floor.

3. **Measure** Use the other ruler to find the distance the paper moved. Record the number.

4. Repeat steps 2 and 3 using a block, a pencil, and a marble.

5. Which object traveled the greatest distance? The shortest distance?

How Do You Measure Motion?

Look again at the snails on page E6. You know the snail moved because it changed position. While an object changes position, it is in **motion** (MOH·shuhn). Motion is a change in position.

Look at the cheetah in the diagram. As it runs the cheetah is in motion. It travels a distance from the start to the finish. It changes direction. Finally, its motion stops. Some motions, such as those of a moving snail, are very slow. Other motions, such as those of a cheetah, are fast. Some motions are very fast.

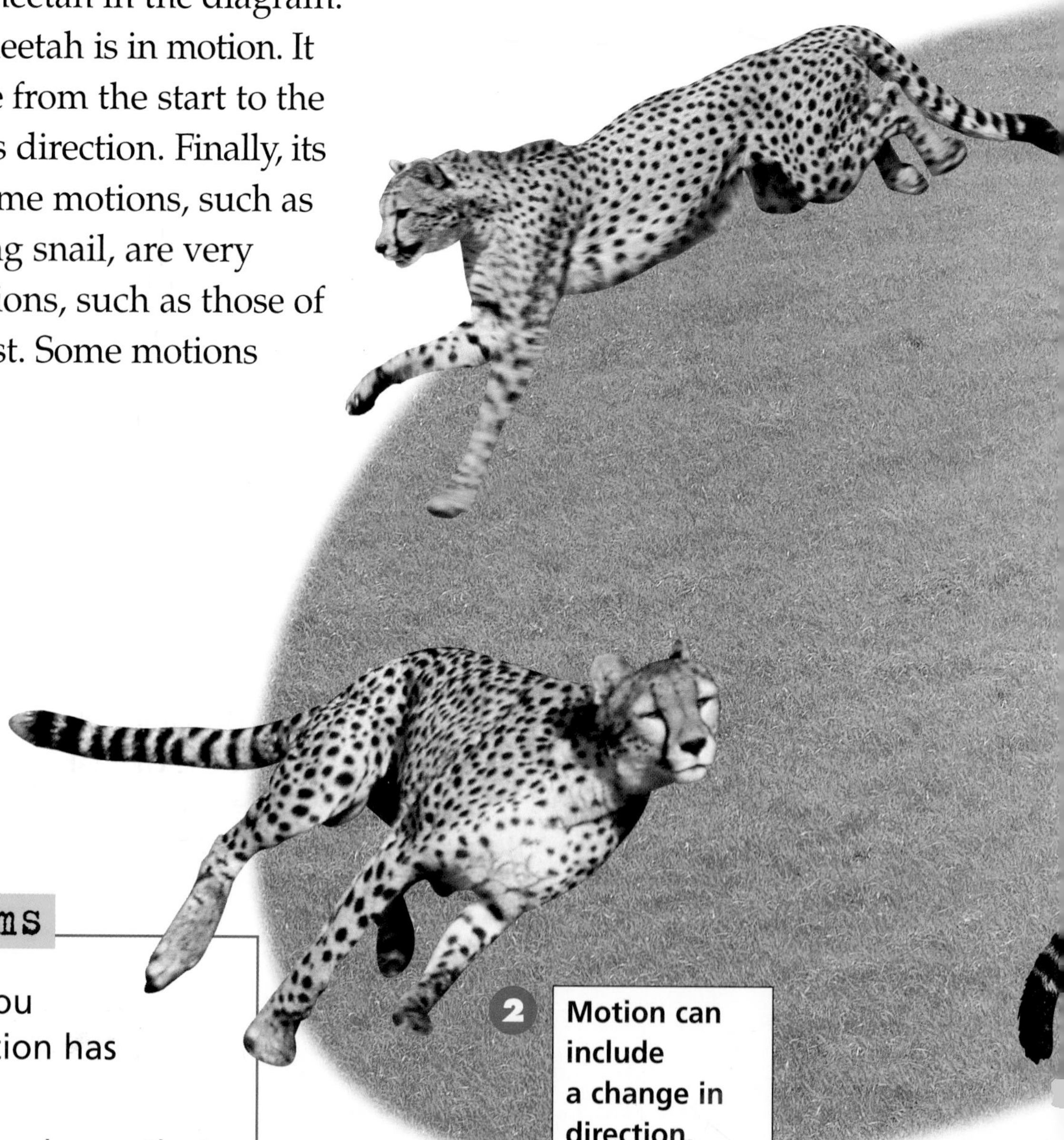

1 Motion takes time to happen.

2 Motion can include a change in direction.

READING
Diagrams

1. How do you know motion has stopped?

2. How do you know that the cheetah moved?

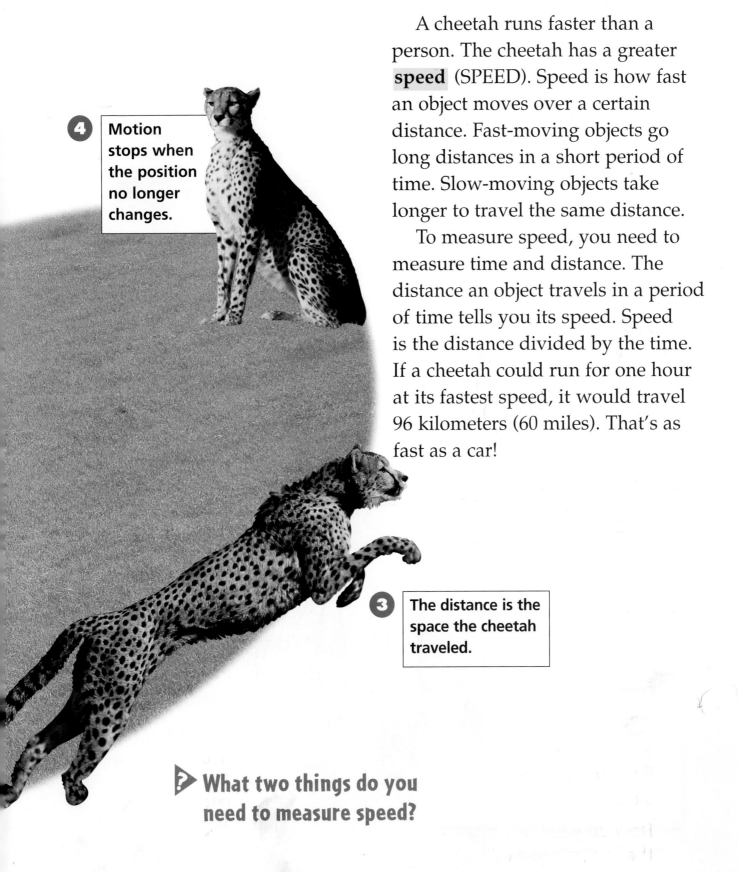

A cheetah runs faster than a person. The cheetah has a greater **speed** (SPEED). Speed is how fast an object moves over a certain distance. Fast-moving objects go long distances in a short period of time. Slow-moving objects take longer to travel the same distance.

To measure speed, you need to measure time and distance. The distance an object travels in a period of time tells you its speed. Speed is the distance divided by the time. If a cheetah could run for one hour at its fastest speed, it would travel 96 kilometers (60 miles). That's as fast as a car!

4 Motion stops when the position no longer changes.

3 The distance is the space the cheetah traveled.

▷ **What two things do you need to measure speed?**

E 9

What Do Maps Tell You?

A map is a flat drawing. It shows the positions of things. To read a map, you need to use directions. Directions include north (N), south (S), east (E), and west (W). Directions are shown below. Every map shows which way is north. This helps you find places or things.

A map also has a key. A key shows what different symbols stand for. The symbol of the purple circle shows a Picnic area.

Look at the map. The Panda House is north of the Pool. The Pool is west of the Picnic area.

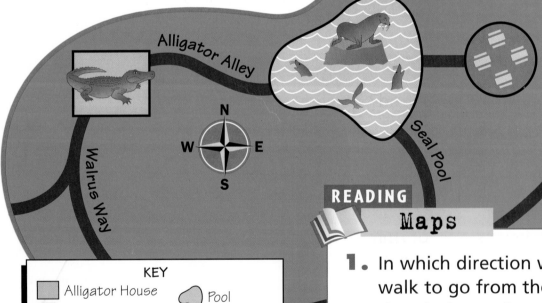

KEY

■ Alligator House
■ Panda House
■ Rhinoceros House
● Pool
● Picnic area

▷ **What does the map key show?**

READING
Maps

1. In which direction would you walk to go from the pool to the picnic area?

2. Plan routes from different places on the map. In which direction would you go to get from each place to another?

Why It Matters

Every day your life is filled with motion. For example, you might move from home to school on the school bus. As it is in motion, the bus travels a distance. If you know the distance and the time the bus traveled, you can find its speed.

Visit **www.mhscience02.com** to do a research project on speed and motion.

Think and Write

1. How would you describe an object that has changed position?

2. How is distance measured?

3. What is motion?

4. Three children live on the same street. Ann lives west of Peter. Peter lives east of Talia. Talia lives west of Ann. Draw a map of their street.

5. **Critical Thinking** Which moves faster—a cheetah running 96 kilometers in an hour or a bicycle traveling 24 kilometers in 30 minutes?

L·I·N·K·S

WRITING LINK

Describe a position. Place three objects in a group. Don't let your partner see them. Describe their positions. Use words like *above, below, left, right, ahead,* and *behind.* Have your partner try to arrange the objects the same way. Switch roles, and try it again. Write down some strategies you discovered.

LITERATURE LINK

Read *There and Back, Then and Now* to learn about the history of travel. When you finish reading, think about your favorite way to travel. Try the activities at the end of the book.

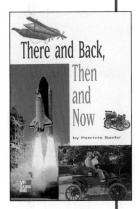

There and Back, Then and Now
by Patricia Baehr

MATH LINK

Solve a problem. If an adult runs 6 miles in an hour, how far will this person travel in 90 minutes? Show your answer. Explain how you solved the problem.

TECHNOLOGY LINK

At the Computer Visit **www.mhscience02.com** for more links.

Forces

Vocabulary

force, E14
gravity, E16
weight, E17

Get Ready

Every day, people use pushes and pulls to move things. In certain parts of the world, farmers use strong animals to pull heavy farm tools. You use a pull when you open a book. What are some other activities that use pushes and pulls?

Process Skill

You measure when you find the weight of an object.

Explore Activity

Why Are Some Objects Harder to Pull?

Materials

spring scale

safety goggles

5 objects
of about the
same size

Procedure

BE CAREFUL! Wear goggles.

1 **Observe** What is the highest the spring scale can read?

2 **Predict** Which object will need the strongest pull to move it? Record your prediction.

3 **Predict** Which object will need the next strongest pull to move it? Record your prediction. Do the same for the rest of the objects.

4 Hook the scale on an object. Pull the scale and the object along a smooth, flat surface.

5 **Measure** Measure and record what the spring scale reads. Do the same for all the objects.

6 Compare your predictions with your measurements.

Drawing Conclusions

1 What did you feel when you pulled on an object with the spring scale?

2 Which objects made the scale read highest?

3 Why did you need a stronger pull to move some objects?

4 **Going Further: Experiment** How could you measure the size of the pull needed to move a lunchbox?

Main Idea You use forces to move things.

What Are Pushes and Pulls?

You push and pull on things every day to make them move. You push to open a door. You pull to put on your backpack.

All pushes and pulls are **forces** (FAWRS·uhz). Forces always work in pairs. When you push on something, such as a door, you can feel it pushing back.

Often a force can change an object's motion. It can make an object start moving, stop moving, or change direction. As you add force to a door, it moves. Sometimes an object doesn't move. No matter how hard you push, you can't push over a brick wall.

Heavier objects need more force to make them move. You have to push or pull a heavier object harder to make it move.

▷ **What do you feel when you push something?**

1 *All pushes and pulls are forces.* Pushes move away from you. Pulls move toward you.

2 *Forces may change the motion of an object.* The heavier an object, the more force you need to move it.

Facts About Forces

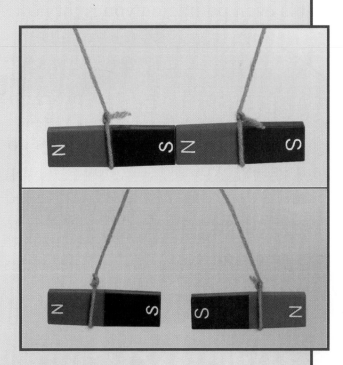

4 *Many things can create forces. Some forces push or pull on objects without even touching them.*

3 *Forces work in pairs.* Whenever you push or pull on something, it pushes or pulls on you. The push or pull that you feel is a force in the opposite direction.

READING Diagrams

1. What is a force?

2. Do you need more or less force to move a heavier object?

What Force Is Always Pulling on You?

One force is everywhere on Earth. It is even pulling on you right now. The force is **gravity** (GRAV·i·tee). Gravity is a pulling force between two objects, such as you and Earth.

This force keeps objects pulled toward Earth. Even when things go up, gravity pulls them down. Things fall to Earth because they are pulled by Earth's gravity.

Performing tasks in space is quite an experience for this astronaut.

READING **Main Idea**
When you jump up, why do you come down?

What Is Weight?

The pull of gravity is just about the same all over Earth. **Weight** (WAYT) is how much pull gravity has on an object.

That means an object's weight will be about the same anywhere on Earth. On other planets and the Moon, the pull of gravity is different. This is why objects have different weights away from Earth.

You can find out how heavy or light things are by measuring their weight. Some objects are heavy. Some are light. Scientists measure weight in *newtons*. A newton is the unit of force in the metric system. In the English system of measurement, the unit is the *pound*.

▷ **Would you weigh the same amount on the Moon?**

The pull of gravity is less on the Moon than on Earth.

These apples weigh nine newtons, or two pounds.

Process Skill
BUILDER

Read a Bar Graph

The graph below is a bar graph. Each bar gives you information, or *data*. This bar graph shows a dog's weight on different planets. Along the left side are the planet names. At the bottom are weights in pounds. Look at the end of the bar labeled *Earth*. It lines up with 40 pounds. The dog weighs 40 pounds on Earth. Look at the bar labeled *Jupiter*. What number does it line up with? You are interpreting data when you answer this question.

Interpret the data in this graph. Use the data to answer the questions.

Procedure

1. **Interpret Data** How much does the dog weigh on Mars?

2. **Interpret Data** Where is the dog heavier than it is on Earth? Where is it lighter?

3. Compare the dog's weight on Jupiter with its weight on Venus. How much heavier is it on Jupiter?

Drawing Conclusions
Communicate How would your weight change if you visited the other planets?

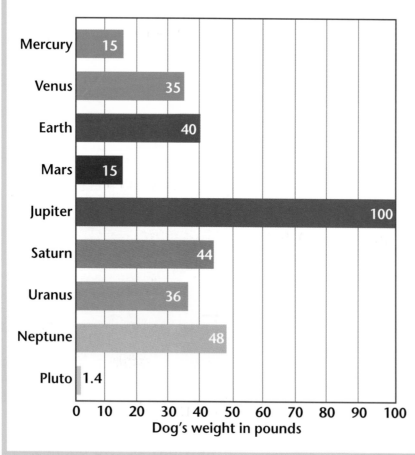

LINKS

Why It Matters

Forces are all around you. Whether you throw a ball, pull a wagon, or push open a door, you are using forces to move things. You use another kind of force when you use a magnet. The force of gravity holds things down on Earth. Gravity is pulling on you and everything else on Earth all the time.

Think and Write

1. How can you measure pushes and pulls?

2. Name one fact about forces.

3. What is the name of the force that always pulls on you?

4. **Interpret Data** Look at the graph on page E18. How much does the dog weigh on Pluto?

5. **Critical Thinking** You drop a plate on Earth. It breaks into pieces. Would the same thing happen in outer space? Explain your answer.

ART LINK

Make a mobile. Collect five small objects. Use buttons, beads, or anything else you find. Use string to attach these items to a plastic hanger. What do you have to do to get your mobile to balance? How does gravity affect your mobile?

LITERATURE LINK

Read *Get a Grip!* to learn how a group of friends build a soapbox car. When you finish reading, think about building your own soapbox car. Try the activities at the end of the book.

WRITING LINK

Write a story. How would a basketball game change if there was no gravity? Write a story that shows what the game would be like. Illustrate your story. Share it with your classmates.

TECHNOLOGY LINK

At the Computer Visit **www.mhscience02.com** for more links.

SHOW YOUR MUSCLES!

Let's hear it for your muscles! They're what help you move and stay on the go. They help you run and score that touchdown, climb trees, swim and dive, and so much more!

When you push or pull, you use muscles. Some of your muscles come in pairs. Your upper arm has biceps and triceps. Both muscles stretch between a bone in your upper arm and one in your lower arm.

Muscles contract, or get shorter. When your biceps contracts, it pulls on the lower bone. Your lower arm moves up so you can lift objects. How would you carry all your books without biceps?

You use your triceps to push things. When your triceps contracts, your biceps relaxes. Your arm becomes straighter, and you can push down.

How are these children using their muscles?

Want to run a little faster? Hit a ball a little harder? The more you push and pull, the stronger your muscles get.

Walking, jogging, and swimming build up muscles in your whole body. They make many muscles pull against gravity.

Here's how to use gravity to strengthen your muscles.

✓ Increase the amount of weight you pull or push.
✓ Increase the amount of time you push or pull that weight.
✓ Increase how often you push or pull that weight.

Remember that muscles need time to rest between exercise sessions!

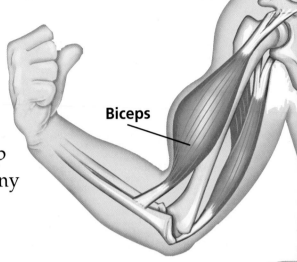

Biceps

Triceps

What Did I Learn?

1. Which activity uses your biceps?

   A walking
   B sitting
   C lifting books
   D pushing down

2. What can you use to strengthen your muscles?

   F friction
   G energy
   H matter
   J gravity

AT THE COMPUTER

Visit **www.mhscience02.com to learn more about your muscles.**

E 21

Changes in Motion

Get Ready

Have you ever played a game of tug-of-war? In this game a flag is tied to the middle of a rope. Each team pulls on the rope. The team that pulls the rope hardest pulls the flag to its side. That team wins. Which team do you think will win?

Process Skill

You experiment when you perform a test to support or disprove a hypothesis.

Explore Activity

What Causes a Change in Motion?

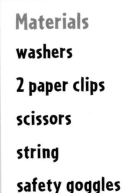

Materials

washers

2 paper clips

scissors

string

safety goggles

Procedure

BE CAREFUL! Wear goggles.

1 Cut two pieces of string that are slightly shorter than the width of your desk. Knot the strings together.

2 Lay the knot in the middle of your desk. Let the strings hang off the opposite sides of the desk.

3 Bend two paper clips into hooks. Tie a hook at the end of each hanging string.

4 Hold down the string at the knot.

5 **Predict** Hang two washers on one hook. Predict what will happen if you let go of the knot.

6 **Experiment** Test your prediction. Record the results.

7 **Experiment** Repeat steps 4, 5, and 6, this time hanging one washer on each hook.

Drawing Conclusions

1 **Communicate** Explain why the knot moved or did not move each time.

2 **Going Further: Form a Hypothesis** How could you move the knot in another direction?

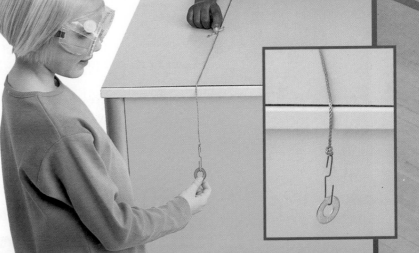

Main Idea Forces can change an object's motion.

What Causes a Change in Motion?

When each person pulls on the rope, each applies a force. When the forces are equal, or balanced, there is no change in motion. The flag stays at rest.

What if one person pulls harder on the end of the rope? The forces are now unequal, or unbalanced. The flag moves to one side of the marker.

Equal forces: no motion

Unequal forces: motion

There is a change in its motion. A change in an object's motion comes from all the forces that are acting on it. Unequal forces cause a change in motion.

A change in motion occurs when an object starts moving or stops moving. It also occurs when a moving object speeds up, slows down, or changes direction. Here are some examples.

❓ What causes a change in motion?

Changes in Motion

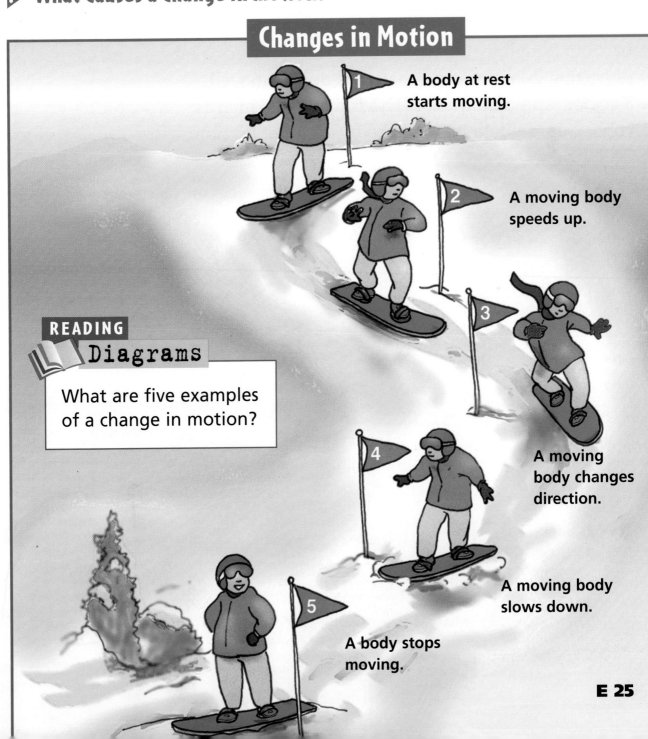

1 A body at rest starts moving.

2 A moving body speeds up.

3 A moving body changes direction.

A moving body slows down.

READING Diagrams

What are five examples of a change in motion?

4

5 A body stops moving.

E 25

Why Do Things Stop Moving?

What happens when you roll a ball on the floor? It starts moving quickly but soon slows down. Then it stops. This means a force must be acting on the ball.

The force that slows the ball is called **friction** (FRIK·shuhn). Friction is the force that occurs when one object rubs against another. The ball rubbing on the floor creates friction.

Different materials produce different amounts of friction. Rough materials rub best. They produce a lot of friction. Many smooth materials don't rub well. They produce less friction. Other materials, such as rubber, are smooth but still produce a lot of friction.

Friction keeps the car's rubber tires on the road, even when the road is wet.

Ice reduces the amount of friction. The cars slide.

What objects rub together when you ride a bicycle? Friction slows the bike down even if you are riding on a very smooth sidewalk. You have to keep pedaling to keep the bike in motion.

How do brakes stop a bike's motion? When you squeeze the brake lever, the brake pad presses against the wheel. This creates friction between the brake pad and the rim of the wheel. The wheel slows down. The bike stops.

▷ **How does friction help a bike slow down?**

Bike Brake

Brake Off   **Brake On**

READING
Diagrams

1. What causes the bike to stop?
2. Is friction greater when the brakes are on or off?

QUICK LAB

FOR SCHOOL OR HOME

Marbles in Motion

1. **Observe** Push a wooden block across your desk. Describe how it feels.

2. **Experiment** Place five marbles under a jar lid. Lay the block on top of the lid.

3. **Observe** Push the block across your desk again. How does it feel now?

4. **Explain** how the marbles helped reduce friction.

How Can You Control Friction?

Friction is a force that slows things down. You can't get rid of friction. You can change the amount of friction you have.

People use slippery things to reduce friction. Oil is often put on moving parts of machines. To increase friction, people use rough or sticky things. In-line skates have a rubber pad that skaters use to slow down and stop.

READING **Main Idea**
How can you change friction?

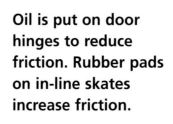

Oil is put on door hinges to reduce friction. Rubber pads on in-line skates increase friction.

Why It Matters

You move objects—and your body—every day. To do so, you use forces. One force that you need and use is friction. Without friction you couldn't grip a doorknob or pick up a ball. You would slip when you tried to walk. Once you were moving, you might not be able to stop!

Think and Write

1. What causes a change in motion?

2. What can you do to move a ball resting on the ground?

3. What is friction?

4. Would it be easier to roller-skate on a gravel road or a smooth road? How do you know?

5. **Critical Thinking** You are swinging on a swing. What must you do to swing higher? What must you do to stop?

L·I·N·K·S

MATH LINK

Make a bar graph. Use the information from the chart below to create a bar graph. Explain why it is easier to compare the data in a bar graph than in the chart. Share this discovery with your teacher.

Stopping Distances		
Ice	Sand	Road
8 meters	1 meter	2 meters

WRITING LINK

Write a story. Write a story about this game. Use the words *motion*, *force*, and *friction* in your story.

TECHNOLOGY LINK

Science Newsroom CD-ROM Choose *Roll Over* to learn more about friction and gravity.

At the Computer Visit www.mhscience02.com for more links.

SPEEDY SKINS

The Olympic Games are contests for the world's best athletes. The results of a swim meet at the Olympics can be very close. A winner might win by only a fraction of a second!

Would you believe a swimsuit can give a racer an advantage? Take a look at this swimsuit called the Fastskin™. It is covered in tiny, V-shaped ridges, much like the skin of a shark. As the swimmer moves through the water, the ridges direct water swiftly over the body.

Another suit covers everything except the hands, feet, and head. This suit is very smooth. It warms and squeezes the swimmer's muscles, helping the swimmer move faster. Still another new kind of suit is coated with Teflon®, the same coating that lets food slide off frying pans.

Some people say the new suits make races unfair for those who do not have them. What do you think? Should all racers wear the same kind of swimsuit?

This swimmer is wearing a Fastskin™ swimsuit.

Swimsuits were very different 80 years ago. This swimsuit is made of wool.

The Aquablade™ swimsuit shown below helps swimmers move fast through the water.

What Did I Learn?

1. What is a Fastskin™?

A a shark's skin
B a seal's skin
C a swimsuit
D a coating for a frying pan

2. A Teflon® coating makes things

F rough.
G dry.
H sticky.
J not sticky.

AT THE COMPUTER

Visit www.mhscience02.com to learn more about swimming and other sports.

Chapter 9 Review

Vocabulary

Fill in each blank with the best word from the list.

distance, E7　　**motion,** E8
force, E14　　**position,** E6
friction, E26　**speed,** E9
gravity, E16　　**weight,** E17

1. An object's location is its _____.

2. How fast an object moves is its _____.

3. When you throw a ball in the air, it falls down because of _____.

4. Snow and ice make the ground have less _____.

5. Unbalanced forces cause _____.

6. You can measure how heavy or light something is by measuring its _____.

7. _____ is the space between two objects.

8. A(n) _____ can be a push or a pull.

9. Two things you need to measure speed are time and _____.

10. _____ is a force that slows objects down.

Test Prep

11. You know you have moved if your _____.

   A speed is zero

   B position stays the same

   C position has changed

   D weight is the same

12. Which of the following measures the speed of a car?

   F 30 miles

   G 30 miles per hour

   H 30 hours

   J 30 meters

13. A goose travels 20 kilometers (12 miles) per hour. How many kilometers does it travel in 8 hours?

   A 40 kilometers

   B 80 kilometers

   C 160 kilometers

   D 460 kilometers

14. Which statement about forces is true?

    F All pushes and pulls are forces.

    G Forces work in pairs.

    H Gravity is a force that is always pulling on you.

    J All of the above.

15. Making a playground slide smoother _____.

    A decreases friction

    B decreases speed

    C decreases motion

    D decreases weight

Concepts and Skills

16. **Critical Thinking** Four people are pushing very hard on a large cardboard box. However, the box is not moving. Explain how this can happen.

17. **Reading in Science** How do brakes stop a bike's motion? Write a few short sentences to explain your answer.

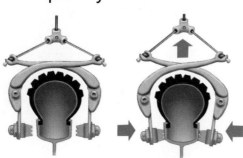

18. **Process Skills: Interpret Data** Who is the fastest runner? Who is the slowest runner? What is the difference in their speed?

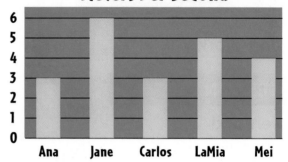

Meters Per Second

19. **Product Ads** Advertisements sometimes show people jumping very high in a certain type of sneakers. What force are these advertisements ignoring? Write a few sentences to explain your answer.

20. **Scientific Methods** Your friend lives in a different country. How could you find out if your friend runs faster than you?

10

LESSON 4

Doing Work, E36

LESSON 5

Levers and
Pulleys, E42

LESSON 6

More Simple
Machines, E52

Work and Machines

Did You Ever Wonder?

Why can you travel faster on a bicycle
than by walking or running? In all three
ways of traveling, you work by moving
your legs up and down. A bicycle makes
work easier. It is a machine made of many
different parts. What are some other
machines, and how do they work?

Doing Work

Vocabulary

work, E38

energy, E39

Get Ready

People often say, "That's a lot of work!" What is work? Look at the picture. One person is doing work. The other person is not doing work. How can you tell who is doing work? Can you do a test to find out?

Process Skill

You classify when you place things that share properties together in groups.

Explore Activity

Materials

4 books

pencil

What Is Work?

Procedure

1 Complete each action described below.
- Pick up one book.
- Pick up four books at one time.
- Put a book on your desk. Push down very hard on top of the book.
- Pick up a pencil from your desk.
- Push against a wall with all of your strength.

2 **Classify** After each action ask yourself, "Did I do work?" Decide whether the action was work. Record your decision in a data chart like the one shown.

Drawing Conclusions

1 Evaluate your answers to the question "Did I do work?" Think about your answers. Is there a pattern? If so, what is it?

2 Explain why you classified each action the way you did. Write a sentence for each action.

3 **Going Further: Classify** Would you classify the following two actions as work or not work? You are listening to music. You are hanging up a jacket.

Action	Work	Conclusion
Pick up one book	Work: Not work:	Why:

Main Idea Work happens when there is a change in motion.

How Are Work and Energy Related?

How would you describe **work**? Scientists say that work is done when a force changes the motion of an object. This means that picking up books *is* work. You apply a force. The motion of the books changes. However, pushing as hard as you can on a wall *is not* work. No matter how hard you push, the wall does not change.

Who's Doing Work?

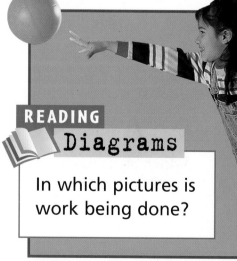

READING Diagrams

In which pictures is work being done?

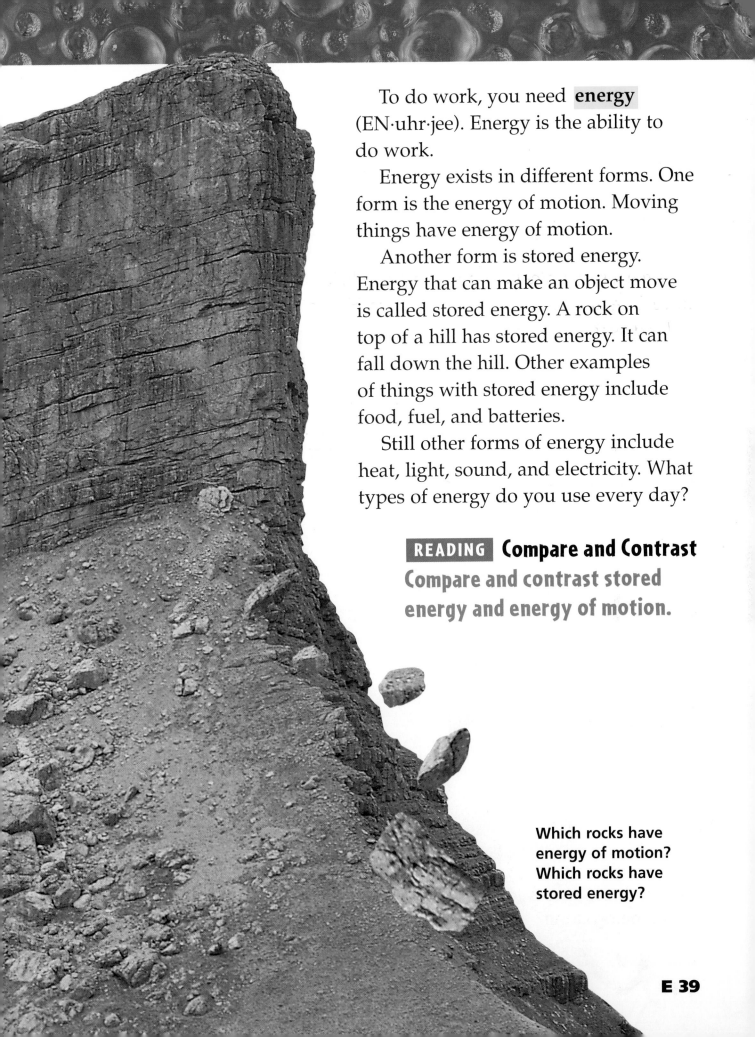

To do work, you need **energy** (EN·uhr·jee). Energy is the ability to do work.

Energy exists in different forms. One form is the energy of motion. Moving things have energy of motion.

Another form is stored energy. Energy that can make an object move is called stored energy. A rock on top of a hill has stored energy. It can fall down the hill. Other examples of things with stored energy include food, fuel, and batteries.

Still other forms of energy include heat, light, sound, and electricity. What types of energy do you use every day?

READING Compare and Contrast

Compare and contrast stored energy and energy of motion.

Which rocks have energy of motion? Which rocks have stored energy?

QUICK LAB

FOR SCHOOL OR HOME

Changing Energy

BE CAREFUL! Wear goggles.

1. Observe Feel the temperature of a block. Describe how it feels.

2. Rub the block with sandpaper about 20 times.

3. Observe Feel the temperature of the block. How does it feel now?

4. What happened to the temperature of the block?

How Does Energy Change?

Energy can change from one form to another. Stored energy can change to the energy of motion when rocks roll down a hill. Another example is friction changing to heat. Try rubbing your hands together for 30 seconds. What do you feel?

Energy can also move from one object to another. Look at the diagram. It shows how energy of motion can move from one ball to another.

▷ **What is one example of how energy can change from one form to another?**

The green ball hits the yellow ball. The force of the green ball causes the yellow ball's motion to change. Now the yellow ball has energy of motion.

Lesson Review

Why It Matters

When people talk about work, they usually mean a job that adults do. Whether you have a job or not, you work every day. You work when you pedal a bike. You work when you jump rope. You even work a little bit when you do your homework! Where do you get the energy to do all this work? You get it from the energy stored in food!

Think and Write

1. Make a list of five things you did today that are examples of work. How do you know each is work?

2. What is energy?

3. How does energy change?

4. What energy change takes place when you hold a heavy box for ten minutes?

5. **Critical Thinking** You swing a baseball bat and hit the ball. The ball goes over the fence. Use the terms *work*, *energy*, *stored energy*, *energy of motion*, and *change of motion* to describe what happened.

L·I·N·K·S

WRITING LINK

Write an expository paragraph. Describe a job you would like to have when you grow up. What kinds of actions would you do in the job you would like to have? Would you be doing a lot of work the way a scientist would describe it?

SOCIAL STUDIES LINK

Research Habitat for Humanity. Habitat for Humanity is a group that helps people work together to build houses. What kinds of work would you do when building a house? Find out about Habitat for Humanity efforts in your area. Write down your findings. Share them with your class.

ART LINK

Make a poster. Our bodies get the energy they need from the food we eat. Think of the foods you eat that give you energy. Make a poster of these foods. Label your drawing. Display the posters about the classroom.

TECHNOLOGY LINK

At the Computer Visit www.mhscience02.com for more links.

Levers and Pulleys

Vocabulary

machine, E44

simple
   machine, E44

lever, E44

wheel and
   axle, E47

pulley, E48

Get Ready

How many machines have you used today? Probably many more than you think. Every day you use machines as you play and work. Machines make our lives easier. Some machines are complex. Others are simple. How do you think machines make work easier?

Process Skill

You experiment when you perform a test to support or disprove a hypothesis.

Explore Activity

How Can You Make Work Easier?

Materials

roll of masking tape

safety goggles

building materials

Procedure: Design Your Own

BE CAREFUL! Wear goggles.

1. Invent a way to get the roll of tape from the floor to your desk. Your hands can help provide the lift, but you can't just pick up the tape.

2. **Communicate** With your group members, think of as many different ways as you can to lift the tape.

3. Write or draw two of your plans. Ask your teacher to approve your plan.

4. **Experiment** Place the roll of masking tape on the floor. Try to lift it. Write down what happens. Does the plan work well?

5. **Experiment** Try another plan for lifting the tape.

Drawing Conclusions

1. Which of your two plans worked better?

2. What materials did you use in your most successful invention?

3. What forces did you use? What force did you work against?

4. **Going Further: Experiment** Would your plan work for lifting a small book? Explain your answer.

Read to Learn

Main Idea Levers and pulleys are machines that make work easier.

How Can You Make Work Easier?

You need to move something. Often you move things with your hands. Sometimes you might need to use a **machine** (muh·SHEEN).

What is a machine? A machine is a tool that makes work easier to do. Remember, work is done when a force changes the motion of an object. How do machines make it easier for forces to move objects? This diagram will help you find out.

A **simple machine** (SIM·puhl muh·SHEEN) is often used to make work easier. Machines with few or no moving parts are called simple machines. A **lever** (LEV·uhr) is an example of a simple machine. A lever is a straight bar that moves on a fixed point. All levers have three important parts—the load, the fulcrum, and the force.

A lever makes moving a load easier in two ways. It lets you change the direction of a force. It may change the amount of force needed to move something.

Look at the girl on page E45. She presses down on one end of the lever. The rock is lifted at the other end. By using the lever, she makes lifting the rock easier.

The load is the object being lifted or moved. The force is the push or pull that moves the lever. The fulcrum is the point where the lever turns.

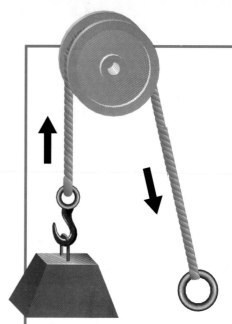

1 A machine can change the direction of the force you need to do work.

▷ **What is a simple machine?**

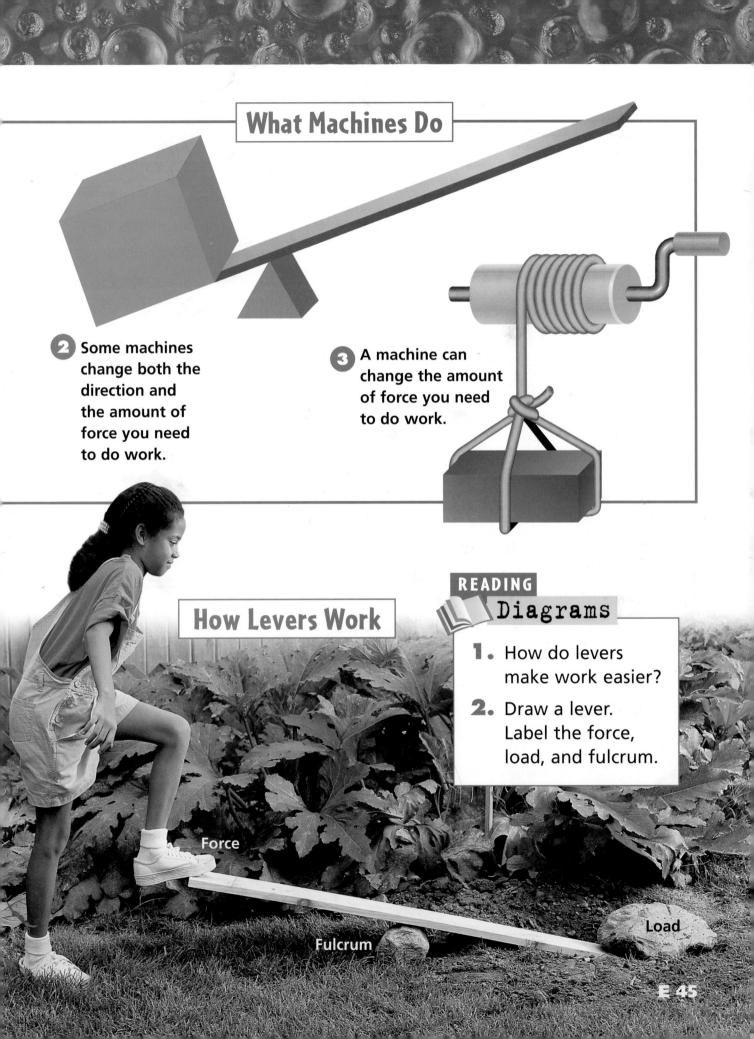

What Machines Do

2 Some machines change both the direction and the amount of force you need to do work.

3 A machine can change the amount of force you need to do work.

How Levers Work

Force

Fulcrum

Load

READING Diagrams

1. How do levers make work easier?

2. Draw a lever. Label the force, load, and fulcrum.

E 45

QUICK LAB

Make a Lever

1. Use clay to hold a pencil in place on your desk.

2. Place a ruler over the center of the pencil.

3. **Experiment** Put two blocks on one end of the ruler. Add pieces of clay to the other end of the ruler. How much clay does it take to lift the blocks?

4. **Experiment** Change the position of the ruler on the pencil. Repeat step 3. How does the new position change your results?

5. Draw your lever. Label the force, load, and fulcrum.

Are There Different Kinds of Levers?

All the levers in the world fall into three types. Each type is set up differently. The force, fulcrum, and load can change places. How the force, fulcrum, and load are arranged tells you what the type of lever is. Take a look at how each lever works.

▶ **What three parts must every lever have?**

Different Kinds of Levers

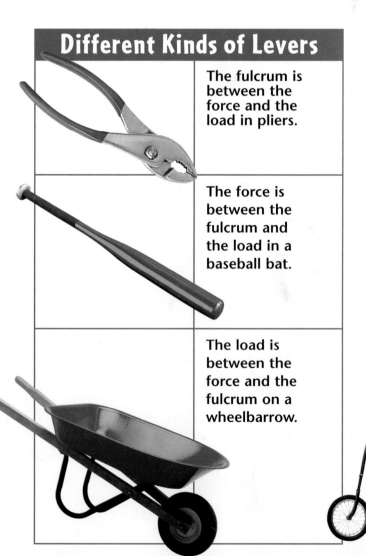

	The fulcrum is between the force and the load in pliers.
	The force is between the fulcrum and the load in a baseball bat.
	The load is between the force and the fulcrum on a wheelbarrow.

What Are Some Other Simple Machines?

Another kind of simple machine is the **wheel and axle** (HWEEL AND AK·suhl). This simple machine has a wheel that turns on a post. The post is called an axle.

A wheel and axle makes work easier. It changes the strength of a turning force. The wheel turns a long distance. The axle turns a short distance.

A *windlass* (WIND·luhs) is used to raise water from a well. A bucket is tied to a rope. The other end of the rope is tied to the axle. At the end of the axle is the handle. When you turn the handle in a large circle, the axle turns in a small circle. The bucket moves up.

> ### How does a wheel and axle make work easier?

Turning the pedals turns the axle. That turns the wheel. When the wheel makes a circle, it goes a long distance.

Handle

Axle

What kind of simple machine is a windlass?

The axle makes a small movement.

The wheel makes a large movement.

What Goes Down to Go Up?

Another simple machine is the **pulley** (POOL·ee). A pulley uses a wheel and a rope to lift a load. There are different kinds of pulleys. The diagram helps you compare two kinds of pulleys you may have seen. In both kinds of pulleys, you pull down to lift up.

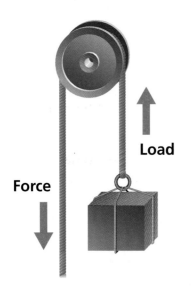

One-wheel pulley

Load

Force

The force and load are equal.

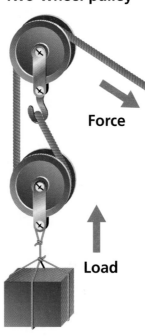

Two-wheel pulley

Force

Load

Less force is needed to move the load.

READING **Compare and Contrast**
Compare two different kinds of pulleys. How are they the same? How are they different?

Why It Matters

You are surrounded by machines. If you don't believe it, take a look around. A spoon is a type of lever. A bottle opener is a type of lever, too. Even your arms, legs, and fingers are levers! What kind of simple machine do you see here?

Think and Write

1. How do machines make work easier?

2. What is a simple machine?

3. What kind of simple machine will help you raise a sail on a sailboat?

4. How do your arms, legs, and fingers help you to lift things during the day?

5. **Critical Thinking** What if you are trying to lift a toy car using a lever? Where can the fulcrum be moved to lift the load most easily?

L·I·N·K·S

SOCIAL STUDIES LINK

Research Archimedes. Archimedes lived in ancient Greece. He was the first to explain how levers work. Use research materials and the Internet to find out more about his life. Write down your findings. Share them with your teacher.

MATH LINK

Make a bar graph. List what types of things you lifted in two days. How many times a day did you lift each? Make a bar graph to show your findings. Share this with your classmates.

LITERATURE LINK

Read *Machines That Build* to learn about simple machines at a construction site. When you finish reading the book, draw your favorite piece of construction equipment. Try the activities at the end of the book.

Machines That Build
by Whit Fisher
illustrated by John Rice

TECHNOLOGY LINK

At the Computer Visit www.mhscience02.com for more links.

Simple Machines
ON A PLAYGROUND

Push off! You rise high in the air. Then down you come. Up and down you go on a simple machine—a seesaw! You don't think about working on a machine. You're having too much fun!

A seesaw is a lever. Look at the picture. Can you find the fulcrum? Hint: Look under the seesaw.

On a seesaw each person sits on one end of the lever. The lever makes it easy to move up and down.

You use another kind of lever when you play baseball. The bat and the batter's arm work together as a lever. The fulcrum is the batter's shoulder. This lever sends the baseball soaring!

Can you find the fulcrum in this photo?

What simple machine is the batter using?

Look at the photograph below. What kind of simple machine do you see? You see a wheel and axle. A child in a wheelchair can roll on a sidewalk without help.

A slide is an example of an inclined plane. You climb to the top, then slide down. This simple machine gives you a fun ride!

What Did I Learn?

1. A baseball bat works as a kind of

A lever.
B inclined plane.
C pulley.
D wheel.

2. A ramp is a kind of

F lever.
G inclined plane.
H pulley.
J wheel.

AT THE COMPUTER

Visit www.mhscience02.com to learn more about simple machines.

More Simple Machines

Vocabulary

ramp, E54

inclined plane, E54

wedge, E55

screw, E56

compound machine, E57

Get Ready

This pyramid is called the Pyramid of the Sun. It was built more than one thousand years ago. It is made from mud, dirt, and large pieces of stone. It stands more than 200 feet tall!

One thousand years ago, there were no bulldozers, tractors, or trucks. People built this huge pyramid. How did they do it?

Process Skill

You infer when you form ideas from facts or observations.

Explore Activity

How Can a Ramp Make Work Easier?

Procedure

BE CAREFUL! Wear goggles.

1. Tie one end of the string around the bottom of the spring scale. Tie the other end to the middle of the spiral wire of the notebook.

2. **Measure** Measure the pull needed to lift the notebook straight up to the height of the chair's seat. Then measure the distance you pulled the book. Record your measurements.

3. Lean one end of the wooden board on the chair.

4. **Measure** Measure the pull needed to move the notebook up the board to the seat of the chair. Then measure the distance you pulled the book. Record your measurements.

5. **Experiment** Adjust the board so it is at a steeper angle. Repeat step 4.

Drawing Conclusions

1. Look at your measurements. Which method of moving the notebook required more force?

2. Which method required moving the notebook a greater distance?

3. **Going Further: Infer** Which method would you use to put a stuffed animal on a shelf? Which method would you use to put a bike on a truck?

Materials

1-m wooden board

spring scale

thin spiral notebook

10-cm piece of string

chair

meterstick

safety goggles

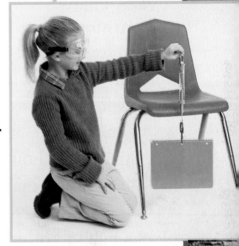

Read to Learn

Main Idea Simple machines make work easier.

What Is an Inclined Plane?

How might the people who built the Pyramid of the Sun have lifted the blocks of stone? They might have used a **ramp**. A ramp is a flat surface that is higher at one end. A ramp is also called an **inclined plane** (in·KLIGHND PLAYN). Inclined planes are simple machines that make work easier.

How does an inclined plane make work easier? To go up a hill, you have two paths. The path that goes straight up is shorter. However, it takes more effort. The ramp is a longer distance, but it takes less effort.

Which way should you go? When the load isn't heavy, you may choose to go straight up. When the load is heavy, you must use a ramp. The stone blocks used to build the pyramid were too heavy to move straight up. Scientists think that they may have been moved using an inclined plane.

Where have you seen ramps used in your community?

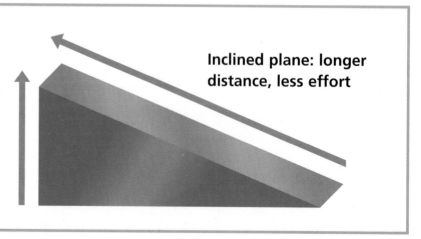

Straight up: shorter distance, more effort

Inclined plane: longer distance, less effort

READING
Diagrams

How do ramps make work easier for people?

A **wedge** (WEJ) is another simple machine. A wedge is made of two inclined planes placed back to back. A wedge uses force to raise an object or to split objects apart.

An ax is a wedge. When an ax is swung, the downward force is changed into a sideways force. The sideways force pushes, or splits, the wood apart.

Another example of a wedge is a plow. A plow is a machine used by farmers. As the plow is dragged through the soil, it cuts through the ground. The soil is pushed aside.

> **What kind of simple machine is a plow?**

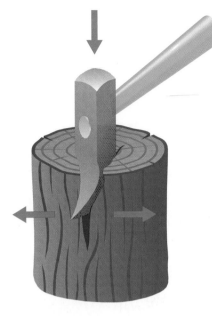

The downward force of the ax changes to the sideways force that splits the wood.

A plow helps a farmer prepare the ground for planting.

What Is a Screw?

What happens when you wrap an inclined plane around a pole? You have a **screw**! A screw is an inclined plane wrapped into a spiral. The ridges of the screw are called *threads*.

It takes less force to turn a screw than to pound a nail. That is because the screw is moving a longer distance. Remember, the longer the distance, the less force you need to do work. When you turn the head of a screw once, the threads travel a long way. You apply force over a longer distance, just like any other inclined plane.

▷ **What simple machine is wrapped around a screw?**

This machine is called an auger. An auger is a screw. It can drill into a rock.

READING Diagrams

1. How do a nail and a screw compare?

2. Which screw has a longer inclined plane?

A screw with a longer inclined plane has more threads. A screw with a shorter inclined plane has fewer threads.

What Happens If You Put Two Simple Machines Together?

You can make work easier by using a **compound machine**, too. When you put two or more simple machines together, you make a compound machine.

A pair of scissors is a compound machine. Part is a lever. Part is a wedge.

A water faucet is also a compound machine. Part is a wheel and axle. Part is a screw.

READING **Compare and Contrast**
How are simple machines and compound machines alike? How are they different?

A bicycle uses wheels and axles, and a lever. There are several sets of wheels and axles.

Process Skill BUILDER

Which Screw Makes Work Easiest?

You know that a screw is a simple machine. It makes work easier, just like any other inclined plane. It lets you use less force over a longer distance. Screws come in many shapes and sizes. Some screws make work easier than others.

The diagram here shows three screws. In this activity you will use numbers to evaluate how each screw is different. Then you will use that information to infer which screw makes work the easiest.

Procedure
1. **Measure** What is the width of each screw's head? What is the length of each screw?

2. Record your measurements in a table.

3. **Use Numbers** Count the number of threads on each screw.

4. Record the information in a table.

Drawing Conclusions
1. How does the number of threads on each screw compare?

2. Explain how the number of threads on each screw relates to the length of its inclined plane.

3. **Infer** Which screw makes work easiest? How do you know?

Materials
ruler

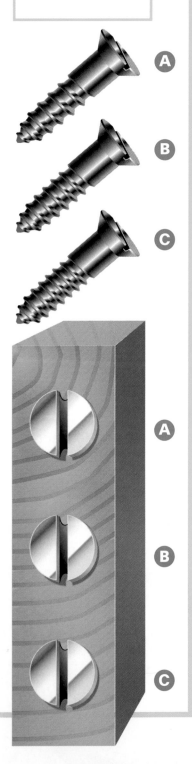

L·I·N·K·S

Why It Matters

Simple and compound machines help you do many of your everyday activities. They help you cut an apple and wrap a present. You use them to travel from place to place. Visit **www.mhscience02.com** to do a research project on simple and compound machines.

Think and Write

1. How does an inclined plane make work easier?

2. What is a compound machine?

3. Which is easier, turning a screw or pounding a nail of the same size? Why?

4. Use Numbers You have two screws. Each measures 2 inches long and has a 1-inch head. One screw has 20 threads. The other screw has 30 threads. Which screw will make work easier? Why?

5. Critical Thinking You see a bird flying by with grass in its beak. Explain how the bird is using its beak as a simple machine.

SOCIAL STUDIES LINK

Take a survey. What simple machines are in your neighborhood? Make a list of the simple machines you find and where they are located. For example, you might see a see saw in the playground.

WRITING LINK

Write an expository paragraph. What if a simple or compound machine you used today did not exist? Write about how you would have done the work. How much harder would the work have been? Share your paragraph with your teacher.

TECHNOLOGY LINK

Science Newsroom CD-ROM Choose *Machines in Motion* to learn about six simple machines.

At the Computer Visit **www.mhscience02.com** for more links.

Chapter 10 Review

Vocabulary

Fill in the blank with the best word or words from the list.

compound machine, E57
inclined plane, E54
lever, E44
machine, E44
pulley, E48
screw, E56
simple machine, E44
wedge, E55
wheel and axle, E47
work, E38

1. A ramp is a type of _____.

2. A(n) _____ is made up of at least two simple machines.

3. When you use a force to change the motion of an object, you do _____.

4. A(n) _____ is a tool that makes work easier to do.

5. The simple machine with a fulcrum, load, and force is a(n) _____.

6. A machine with few or no moving parts is a(n) _____.

Two types of inclined planes:

7. _____

8. _____.

Two types of levers:

9. _____

10. _____.

Test Prep

11. Which is a true statement about work?

   A Work takes money.

   B Work takes a long time.

   C Work changes an object's size.

   D Work changes an object's position.

12. A lever moves back and forth on a(n) _____.

   F fulcrum

   G straight bar

   H axle

   J ramp

13. What simple machine is shown in the diagram?

   A wheel and axle

   B screw

   C inclined plane

   D lever

14. Which simple machine lets a roller skate roll?

   F a screw

   G a pulley

   H an inclined plane

   J a wheel and axle

15. A pair of scissors is a compound machine. What two simple machines make up a pair of scissors?

   A wheel and axle, and lever

   B lever and wedge

   C lever and pulley

   D pulley and wedge

Concepts and Skills

16. **Reading in Science** Look at the two different types of pulleys below. How are they alike? How are they different?

One-wheel pulley   **Two-wheel pulley**

17. **Critical Thinking** Amanda can lift 10 kilograms with a single pulley. Will a two-pulley system make lifting easier? Explain your answer.

18. **Process Skills: Use Numbers** You want to pry a big rock out of your garden. You have a 1-meter board and a 2-meter board. Which board will help you move the rock more easily? Explain.

19. **Scientific Methods** You are asked to design a roller coaster. You need to find a way to make the cars go faster down an inclined plane. Describe how you would test your ideas.

20. **Decision Making** There is a meeting in your school to discuss plans to install ramps for people with disabilities. You have been asked to speak. Write a speech explaining what you would say.

Boost your test scores!

Be Smart!
Visit www.mhscience02.com **to learn more.**

People in Science

Dr. Kalpana Chawla
Engineer and Astronaut

Dr. Kalpana Chawla

Three . . . two . . . one . . . liftoff! The space shuttle is off on another flight into space. But how can things move in space? There are no roads or tracks. There are no traffic signs. There's not even any air! It's the job of the aerospace engineers at NASA to get the shuttle into space. And to get it back down again!

One of NASA's aerospace engineers is Dr. Kalpana Chawla. Dr. Chawla was born in India and grew up with dreams of becoming an astronaut. She was hired by NASA in 1988 to do research in space aircraft propulsion. Propulsion is getting things moving and keeping them moving.

Her dream came true. She was chosen by NASA to become an astronaut on the space shuttle. In 1997 she spent 16 days in space. One of Dr. Chawla's jobs was to conduct experiments. She studied how being weightless during space flight affects the human body. She studied formation of crystals, combustion, and plant growth in micro-gravity.

By the time the mission was over, Dr. Chawla and her crewmates had circled Earth 252 times. They had traveled over six million miles!

Each time the space shuttle goes on a mission, we learn more about what living in space would be like. Do you think you would like living in space?

Dr. Chawla studied how being weightless affects the human body.

Careers IN SCIENCE

Here are some different types of careers related to the study of space travel. You can use the Internet or library resources to find out more about these careers.

- pilot
- astronomer
- medical researcher
- physicist
- space shuttle mechanic

Aerospace engineers help get the space shuttle into outer space.

Write ABOUT IT

1. What is the job of an aerospace engineer?
2. Imagine you are an astronaut aboard the space shuttle. What would you want to study? Why?

Gravity Games

Your goal is to build a toy or game that uses gravity.

What to Do

Gravity causes things to fall to Earth. You can roll a marble down a ramp. You can toss a ball into the air and it comes back down. Invent a toy or game that uses gravity. Write down your invention. Have your teacher approve it. Try to build it. You can use materials such as marbles, construction paper, modeling clay, or shoe boxes.

Draw Conclusions

Identify the forces that are used in your toy or game. Write them down.

Machines Make an Amusement Park Fun!

Your goal is to make a model of a ride at an amusement park.

What to Do

Remember the rides at an amusement park? Use what you've learned about machines and forces to build your own ride. Use materials such as rubber bands, paper plates, milk cartons, and crayons.

Draw Conclusions

Write a short paragraph to explain what type of machine you built and what type of force it uses.

For Your Reference

Science Handbook

Units of Measurement . . . . R 2

Use a Hand Lens . . . . R 4

Use a Microscope . . . . R 5

Measure Time . . . . R 6

Measure Length . . . . R 7

Measure Mass . . . . R 8

Measure Volume . . . . R 9

Measure Weight/Force . . . . R 10

Measure Temperature . . . . R 11

Use Calculators . . . . R 12

Use Computers . . . . R 14

Make Graphs to Organize Data . . . . R 16

Make Maps, Tables, Charts . . . . R 18

Health Handbook

The Skeletal System . . . . R 20

The Muscular System . . . . R 23

The Circulatory System . . . . R 24

The Respiratory System . . . . R 26

Activity Pyramid/Food Guide Pyramid . . . . R 27

The Digestive System . . . . R 28

The Excretory System . . . . R 29

The Nervous System . . . . R 30

The Endocrine System . . . . R 31

The Senses . . . . R 32

The Immune System . . . . R 34

Glossary

Glossary . . . . R 35

Index

Index . . . . R 49

Units of Measurement

Temperature

1. The temperature is 77 degrees Fahrenheit.

2. That is the same as 25 degrees Celsius.

3. Water boils at 212 degrees Fahrenheit.

4. Water freezes at 0 degrees Celsius.

Length and Area

1. This classroom is 10 meters wide and 20 meters long.

2. That means the area is 200 square meters.

Mass and Weight

1. That baseball bat weighs 32 ounces.

2. 32 ounces is the same as 2 pounds.

3. The mass of the bat is 907 grams.

Measurement

Volume of Fluids

Weight/Force

Rate

1. This bottle of juice has a volume of 1 liter.

2. That is a little more than 1 quart.

3. I weigh 85 pounds. That is a force of 380.8 newtons.

1. She can walk 20 meters in 5 seconds.

2. That means her speed is 4 meters per second.

Table of Measurements

SI (International System) of Units	English System of Units
Temperature Water freezes at 0 degrees Celsius (°C) and boils at 100°C.	**Temperature** Water freezes at 32 degrees Fahrenheit (°F) and boils at 212°F.
Length and Distance 10 millimeters (mm) = 1 centimeter (cm) 100 centimeters = 1 meter (m) 1,000 meters = 1 kilometer (km)	**Length and Distance** 12 inches (in.) = 1 foot (ft) 3 feet = 1 yard (yd) 5,280 feet = 1 mile (mi)
Volume 1 cubic centimeter (cm³) = 1 milliliter (mL) 1,000 milliliters = 1 liter (L)	**Volume of Fluids** 8 fluid ounces (fl oz) = 1 cup (c) 2 cups = 1 pint (pt) 2 pints = 1 quart (qt) 4 quarts = 1 gallon (gal)
Mass 1,000 milligrams (mg) = 1 gram (g) 1,000 grams = 1 kilogram (kg)	**Weight** 16 ounces (oz) = 1 pound (lb) 2,000 pounds = 1 ton (T)
Area 1 square kilometer (km²) =1 km x 1 km 1 hectare = 10,000 square meters (m²)	**Rate** mph = miles per hour
Rate m/s = meters per second km/h = kilometers per hour	
Force 1 newton (N) = 1 kg x 1m/s²	

Use a Hand Lens

You use a hand lens to magnify an object, or make the object look larger. With a hand lens, you can see details that would be hard to see without the hand lens.

Magnify a Piece of Cereal

1. Place a piece of your favorite cereal on a flat surface. Look at the cereal carefully. Draw a picture of it.
2. Hold the hand lens so that it is just above the cereal. Look through the lens, and slowly move it away from the cereal. The cereal will look larger.
3. Keep moving the hand lens until the cereal begins to look blurry. Then move the lens a little closer to the cereal until you can see it clearly.
4. Draw a picture of the cereal as you see it through the hand lens. Fill in details that you did not see before.
5. Repeat this activity using objects you are studying in science. It might be a rock, some soil, a seed, or something else.

Use a Microscope

Hand lenses make objects look several times larger. A microscope, however, can magnify an object to look hundreds of times larger.

Examine Salt Grains

1. Place the microscope on a flat surface. Always carry a microscope with both hands. Hold the arm with one hand, and put your other hand beneath the base.
2. Look at the drawing to learn the different parts of the microscope.
3. Move the mirror so that it reflects light up toward the stage. Never point the mirror directly at the Sun or a bright light. Bright light can cause permanent eye damage.
4. Place a few grains of salt on the slide. Put the slide under the stage clips on the stage. Be sure that the salt grains are over the hole in the stage.
5. Look through the eyepiece. Turn the focusing knob slowly until the salt grains come into focus.
6. Draw what the grains look like through the microscope.
7. Look at other objects through the microscope. Try a piece of leaf, a strand of human hair, or a pencil mark.
8. Draw what each object looks like through the microscope. Do any of the objects look alike? If so, how? Are any of the objects alive? How do you know?

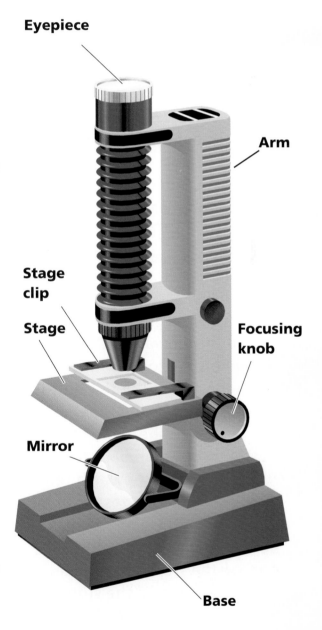

Eyepiece

Arm

Stage clip

Stage

Focusing knob

Mirror

Base

Measure Time

You use timing devices to measure how long something takes to happen. Some timing devices you use in science are a clock with a second hand and a stopwatch. Which one is more accurate?

Comparing a Clock and a Stopwatch

1. Look at a clock with a second hand. The second hand is the hand that you can see moving. It measures seconds.
2. Get an egg timer with falling sand. When the second hand of the clock points to 12, tell your partner to start the egg timer. Watch the clock while the sand in the egg timer is falling.
3. When the sand stops falling, count how many seconds it took. Record this measurement. Repeat the activity, and compare the two measurements.
4. Look at a stopwatch. Click the button on the top right. This starts the time. Click the button again. This stops the time. Click the button on the top left. This sets the stopwatch back to zero. Notice that the stopwatch tells time in hours, minutes, seconds, and hundredths of a second.
5. Repeat the activity in steps 1–3, but use the stopwatch instead of a clock. Make sure the stopwatch is set to zero. Click the top right button to start timing. Click the

button again when the sand stops falling. Make sure you and your partner time the sand twice.

0 minutes   **25 seconds 72 hundredths of a second**

More About Time

1. Use the stopwatch to time how long it takes an ice cube to melt under cold running water. How long does an ice cube take to melt under warm running water?
2. Match each of these times with the action you think took that amount of time.

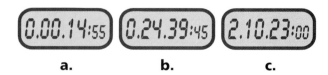

a.   b.   c.

1. A Little League baseball game
2. Saying the Pledge of Allegiance
3. Recess

Measure Length

Find Length with a Ruler

1. Look at this section of a ruler. Each centimeter is divided into 10 millimeters. How long is the paper clip?
2. The length of the paper clip is 3 centimeters plus 2 millimeters. You can write this length as 3.2 centimeters.
3. Place a ruler on your desk. Lay a pencil against the ruler so that one end of the pencil lines up with the left edge of the ruler. Record the length of the pencil.
4. Trade pencils with a classmate. Measure and record the length of each other's pencils. Compare your answers.

Measuring Area

Area is the amount of surface something covers. To find the area of a rectangle, multiply the rectangle's length by its width. For example, the rectangle here is 3 centimeters long and 2 centimeters wide. Its area is 3 cm x 2 cm = 6 square centimeters. You write the area as 6 cm².

1. Find the area of your science book. Measure the book's length to the nearest centimeter. Measure its width.
2. Multiply the book's length by its width. Remember to put the answer in cm².

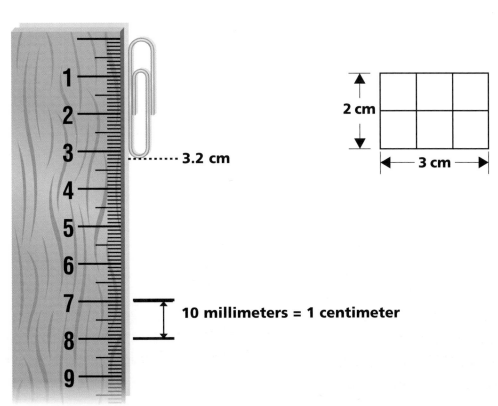

3.2 cm

2 cm

3 cm

10 millimeters = 1 centimeter

Measure Mass

Mass is the amount of matter an object has. You use a balance to measure mass. To find the mass of an object, you balance it with objects whose masses you know. Let's find the mass of a box of crayons.

Measure the Mass of a Box of Crayons

1. Place the balance on a flat, level surface.
2. Make sure the empty pans are balanced with each other. The pointer should point to the middle mark. If it does not, move the slider a little to the right or left to balance the pans.
3. Gently place a box of crayons on the left pan.
4. Add masses to the right pan until the pans are balanced.

5. Count the numbers on the masses that are in the right pan. The total is the mass of the box of crayons, in grams. Record this number. After the number, write a *g* for "grams."

More About Mass

What would happen if you replaced the crayons with a pineapple? You may not have enough masses to balance the pineapple. It has a mass of about 1,000 grams. That's the same as 1 kilogram, because *kilo* means "1,000."

Measure Volume

Have you ever used a measuring cup? Measuring cups measure the volume of liquids. Volume is the amount of space something takes up. In science you use special measuring cups called beakers and graduated cylinders. These containers are marked in milliliters (mL).

Measure the Volume of a Liquid

1. Look at the beaker and at the graduated cylinder. The beaker has marks for each 25 mL up to 200 mL. The graduated cylinder has marks for each 1 mL up to 100 mL.

2. The surface of the water in the graduated cylinder curves up at the sides. You measure the volume by reading the height of the water at the flat part. What is the volume of water in the graduated cylinder? How much water is in the beaker?

3. Pour 50 mL of water from a pitcher into a graduated cylinder. The water should be at the 50-mL mark on the graduated cylinder. If you go over the mark, pour a little water back into the pitcher.

4. Pour the 50 mL of water into a beaker.

5. Repeat steps 3 and 4 using 30 mL, 45 mL, and 25 mL of water.

6. Measure the volume of water you have in the beaker. Do you have about the same amount of water as your classmates?

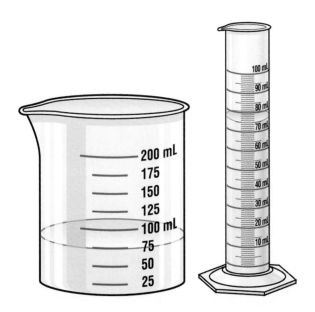

Measure Weight/Force

You use a spring scale to measure weight. An object has weight because the force of gravity pulls down on the object. Therefore, weight is a force. Like all forces, weight is measured in newtons (N).

Measure the Weight of an Object

1. Look at your spring scale to see how many newtons it measures. See how the measurements are divided. The spring scale shown here measures up to 10 N. It has a mark for every 1 N.

2. Hold the spring scale by the top loop. Put the object to be measured on the bottom hook. If the object will not stay on the hook, place it in a net bag. Then hang the bag from the hook.

3. Let go of the object slowly. It will pull down on a spring inside the scale. The spring is connected to a pointer. The pointer on the spring scale shown here is a small arrow.

4. Wait for the pointer to stop moving. Read the number of newtons next to the pointer. This is the object's weight. The mug in the picture weighs 3 N.

More About Spring Scales

You probably weigh yourself by standing on a bathroom scale. This is a spring scale. The force of your body stretches a spring inside the scale. The dial on the scale is probably marked in pounds—the English unit of weight. One pound is equal to about 4.5 newtons.

Here are some spring scales you may have seen.

Measure Temperature

Temperature is how hot or cold something is. You use a thermometer to measure temperature. A thermometer is made of a thin tube with colored liquid inside. When the liquid gets warmer, it expands and moves up the tube. When the liquid gets cooler, it contracts and moves down the tube. You may have seen most temperatures measured in degrees Fahrenheit (°F). Scientists measure temperature in degrees Celsius (°C).

Read a Thermometer

1. Look at the thermometer shown here. It has two scales—a Fahrenheit scale and a Celsius scale. Every 20 degrees on each scale has a number.
2. What is the temperature shown on the thermometer? At what temperature does water freeze? Give your answers in °F and in °C.

How Is Temperature Measured?

1. Fill a large beaker about one-half full of cool water. Find the temperature of the water by holding a thermometer in the water. Do not let the bulb at the bottom of the thermometer touch the sides or bottom of the beaker.
2. Keep the thermometer in the water until the liquid in the tube stops moving— about a minute. Read and record the temperature on the Celsius scale.

3. Fill another large beaker one-half full of warm water from a faucet. Be careful not to burn yourself by using hot water.
4. Find and record the temperature of the warm water just as you did in steps 1 and 2.

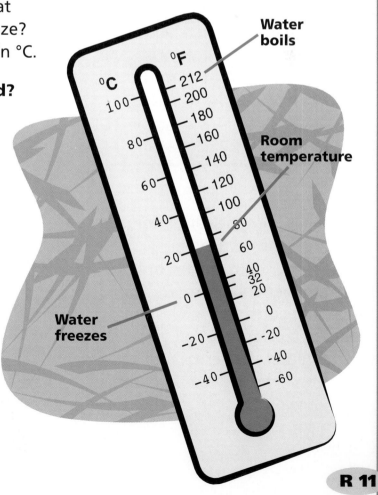

Water boils

Room temperature

Water freezes

Use Calculators: Add and Subtract

Sometimes after you make measurements, you have to add or subtract your numbers. A calculator helps you do this.

Add and Subtract Rainfall Amounts

The table shows the amount of rain that fell in a town each week during the summer.

Week	Rain (cm)
1	3
2	5
3	2
4	0
5	1
6	6
7	4
8	0
9	2
10	2
11	6
12	5

1. Make sure the calculator is on. Press the **ON** key.
2. To add the numbers, enter a number and press ➕. Repeat until you enter the last number. Then press ✚. You do not have to enter the zeros. Your total should be 36.

3. What if you found out that you made a mistake in your measurement? Week 1 should be 2 cm less, week 6 should be 3 cm less, week 11 should be 1 cm less, and week 12 should be 2 cm less. Subtract these numbers from your total. You should have 36 displayed on the calculator. Press ➖, and enter the first number you want to subtract. Repeat until you enter the last number. Then press ✚.

Use Calculators: Multiply and Divide

Sometimes after you make measurements, you have to multiply or divide your measurements to get other information. A calculator helps you multiply and divide, especially if the numbers have decimal points.

Multiply Decimals

What if you are measuring the width of your classroom? You discover that the floor is covered with tiles and the room is exactly 32 tiles wide. You measure a tile, and it is 22.7 centimeters wide. To find the width of the room, you can multiply 32 by 22.7.

1. Make sure the calculator is on. Press the **ON** key.
2. Press **3** and **2**.
3. Press **×**.
4. Press **2**, **2**, **·**, and **7**.
5. Press **=**. Your total should be 726.4. That is how wide the room is in centimeters.

Divide Decimals

Now what if you wanted to find out how many desks placed side by side would be needed to reach across the room? You measure one desk, and it is 60 centimeters wide. To find the number of desks needed, divide 726.4 by 60.

1. Turn the calculator on.
2. Press **7**, **2**, **6**, **·**, and **4**.
3. Press **÷**.
4. Press **6** and **0**.
5. Press **=**. Your total should be about 12.1. This means you can fit 12 desks across the room with a little space left over.

What if the room was 35 tiles wide? How wide would the room be? How many desks would fit across it?

Use Computers

A computer has many uses. The Internet connects your computer to many other computers around the world, so you can collect all kinds of information. You can use a computer to show this information and write reports. Best of all, you can use a computer to explore, discover, and learn.

You can also get information from CD-ROMs. They are computer disks that can hold large amounts of information. You can fit a whole encyclopedia on one CD-ROM.

Use Computers for a Project

Here is how one group of students uses computers as they work on a weather project.

1. The students use instruments to measure temperature, wind speed, wind direction, and other parts of the weather. They input this information, or data, into the computer. The students keep the data in a table. This helps them compare the data from one day to the next.

2. The teacher finds out that another group of students in a town 200 kilometers to the west is also doing a weather project. The two groups use the Internet to talk to each other and share data. When a storm happens in the town to the west, that group tells the other group that it's coming its way.

Use Technology

email: It's going to storm here. The sky is turning dark gray. The winds are sometimes 65 km per hour from the northwest.

3. The students want to find out more. They decide to stay on the Internet and send questions to a local TV weather forecaster. She has a website and answers questions from students every day.

4. Meanwhile some students go to the library to gather more information from a CD-ROM disk. The CD-ROM has an encyclopedia that includes movie clips with sound. The clips give examples of different kinds of storms.

5. The students have kept all their information in a folder called Weather Project. Now they use that information to write a report about the weather. On the computer they can move paragraphs, add words, take out words, put in diagrams, and draw their own weather maps. Then they print the report in color.

6. Use the information on these two pages to plan your own investigation. Use a computer, the Internet, a CD-ROM, or any other technological device.

Make Graphs to Organize Data

When you do an experiment in science, you collect information. To find out what your information means, you can organize it into graphs. There are many kinds of graphs.

Bar Graphs

A bar graph uses bars to show information. For example, what if you are growing a plant? Every week you measure how high the plant has grown. Here is what you find.

Week	Height (cm)
1	1
2	3
3	6
4	10
5	17
6	20
7	22
8	23

The bar graph at right organizes the measurements you collected so that you can easily compare them.

1. Look at the bar for week 2. Put your finger at the top of the bar. Move your finger straight over to the left to find how many centimeters the plant grew by the end of week 2.
2. Between which two weeks did the plant grow most?
3. When did plant growth begin to level off?

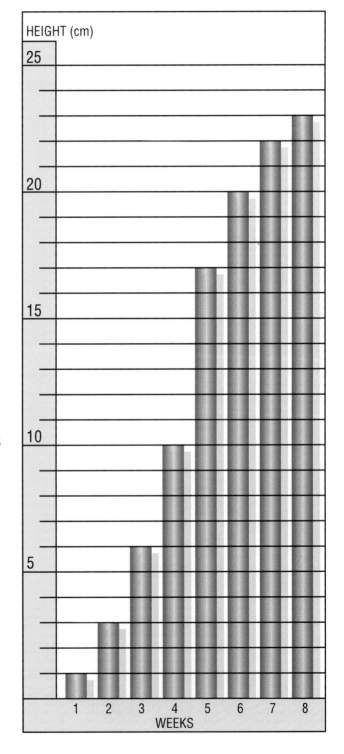

Represent Data

Pictographs

A pictograph uses symbols, or pictures, to show information. What if you collect information about how much water your family uses each day? Here is what you find.

Activity	Water Used Each Day (L)
Drinking	10
Showering	100
Bathing	120
Brushing teeth	40
Washing dishes	80
Washing hands	30
Washing clothes	160
Flushing toilet	50

You can organize this information into the pictograph shown here. In this pictograph each bottle means 20 liters of water. A half bottle means half of 20, or 10 liters of water.

1. Which activity uses the most water?
2. Which activity uses the least water?

Line Graphs

A line graph shows information by connecting dots plotted on the graph. It shows change over time. What if you measure the temperature outdoors every hour starting at 6 A.M.? Here is what you find.

Time	Temperature (°C)
6 A.M.	10
7 A.M.	12
8 A.M.	14
9 A.M.	16
10 A.M.	18
11 A.M.	20

You can organize this information into a line graph. Follow these steps.

1. Make a scale along the bottom and side of the graph. The scales should include all the numbers in the chart. Label the scales.
2. Plot points on the graph.
3. Connect the points with a line.

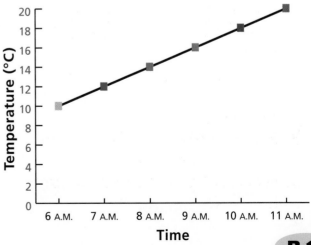

Represent Data

Make Maps, Tables, Charts

Locate Places

A map is a drawing that shows an area from above. Most maps have numbers and letters along the top and side. What if you wanted to find the library on the map below? It is located at D7. Place a finger on the letter D along the side of the map and another finger on the number 7 at the top. Then move your fingers straight across and down the map until they meet. The library is located where D and 7 meet.

1. What building is located at G3?
2. The hospital is located three blocks south and three blocks east of the library. What is its number and letter?
3. Make a map of an area in your community. It might be a park or the area between your home and school. Include numbers and letters along the top and side. Use a compass to find north, and mark north on your map. Exchange maps with classmates.

Idea Maps

The map below left shows how places are connected to each other. Idea maps, on the other hand, show how ideas are connected to each other. Idea maps help you organize information about a topic.

Look at the idea map below. It connects ideas about water. This map shows that Earth's water is either fresh water or salt water. The map also shows four sources of fresh water. You can see that there is no connection between "rivers" and "salt water" on the map. This reminds you that salt water does not flow in rivers.

Make an idea map about a topic you are learning in science. Your map can include words, phrases, or even sentences. Arrange your map in a way that makes sense to you and helps you understand the ideas.

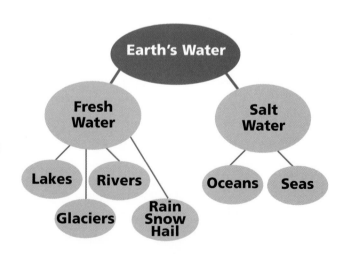

Make Tables and Charts to Organize Data

Tables help to organize data during experiments. Most tables have columns that run up and down, and rows that run across. The columns and rows have headings that tell you what kind of data goes in each part of the table.

A Sample Table

What if you are going to do an experiment to find out how long different kinds of seeds take to sprout? Before you begin the experiment, you should set up your table. Follow these steps.

1. In this experiment you will plant 20 radish seeds, 20 bean seeds, and 20 corn seeds. Your table must show how many of each kind of seed sprouted on days 1, 2, 3, 4, and 5.

2. Make your table with columns, rows, and headings. You might use a computer. Some computer programs let you build a table with just the click of a mouse. You can delete or add columns and rows if you need to.

3. Give your table a title. Your table could look like the one here.

Make a Table

Plant 20 bean seeds in each of two trays. Keep each tray at a different temperature, as shown above, and observe the trays for seven days. Make a table that you can use for this experiment. You can use the table to record, examine, and evaluate the information of this experiment.

Make a Chart

A chart is simply a table with pictures, as well as words to label the rows or columns. Make a chart that shows the information of the above experiment.

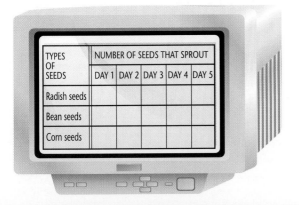

TYPES OF SEEDS	NUMBER OF SEEDS THAT SPROUT				
	DAY 1	DAY 2	DAY 3	DAY 4	DAY 5
Radish seeds					
Bean seeds					
Corn seeds					

The Skeletal System

The body has a supporting frame, called a skeleton, which is made up of bones. The skeleton has several jobs.

- It gives the body its shape.
- It protects organs in the body.
- It works with muscles to move the body.

Each of the 206 bones of the skeleton is the size and shape best fitted to do its job. For example, long and strong leg bones support the body's weight.

CARE!

- Exercise to keep your skeletal system in good shape.
- Don't overextend your joints.

The Skeleton

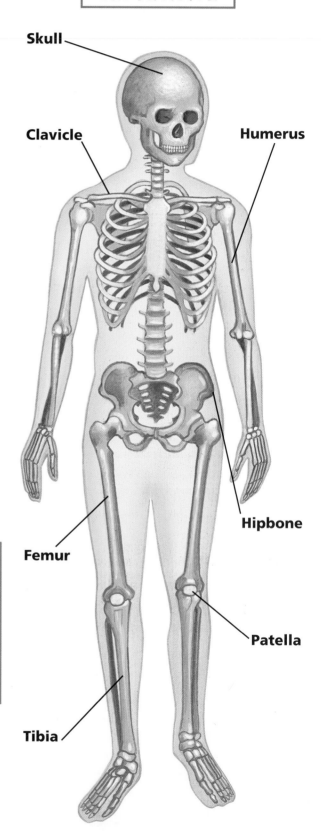

Skull

Clavicle

Humerus

Femur

Hipbone

Patella

Tibia

Bones

1 A bone is covered with a tough but thin membrane that has many small blood vessels. The blood vessels bring nutrients and oxygen to the living parts of the bone and remove wastes.

2 Inside some bones is a soft tissue known as marrow. Yellow marrow is made mostly of fat cells and is one of the body's energy reserves. It is usually found in the long, hollow spaces of long bones.

3 Part of the bone is compact, or solid. It is made up of living bone cells and non-living materials. The nonliving part is made up of layers of hardened minerals such as calcium and phosphorus. In between the mineral layers are living bone cells.

4 Red marrow fills the spaces in spongy bone. Red marrow makes new red blood cells, germ-fighting white blood cells, and cell fragments that stop a cut from bleeding.

5 Part of the bone is made of bone tissue that looks like a dry sponge. It is made of strong, hard tubes. It is also found in the middle of short, flat bones.

CARE!

- **Eat foods rich in vitamins and minerals. Your bones need the minerals calcium and phosphorus to grow strong.**

- **Be careful! Avoid sprains and fractures.**

- **Get help in case of injury.**

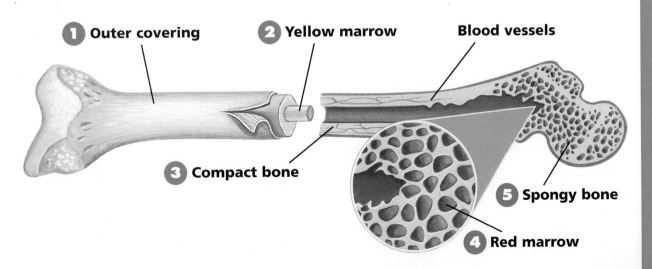

1 Outer covering   **2 Yellow marrow**   **Blood vessels**

3 Compact bone

5 Spongy bone

4 Red marrow

Joints

The skeleton has different types of joints. A joint is a place where two or more bones meet. Joints can be classified into three major groups—immovable joints, partly movable joints, and movable joints.

Types of Joints

IMMOVABLE JOINTS

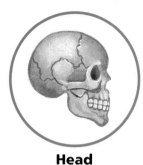

Head

Immovable joints are places where bones fit together too tightly to move. Nearly all the 29 bones in the skull meet at immovable joints. Only the lower jaw can move.

PARTLY MOVABLE JOINTS

Partly movable joints are places where bones can move only a little. Ribs are connected to the breastbone with these joints.

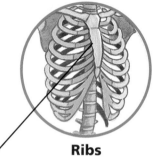

Breastbone

Ribs

MOVABLE JOINTS

Movable joints are places where bones can move easily.

Gliding joint

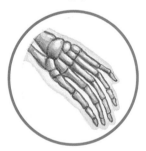

Hand and wrist

Small bones in the wrists and ankles meet at gliding joints. The bones can slide against one another. These joints allow some movement in all directions.

The hips are examples of ball-and-socket joints. The ball of one bone fits into the socket, or cup, of another bone. These joints allow bones to move back and forth, in a circle, and side to side.

Ball-and-socket joint

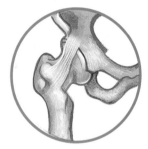

Hip

Hinge joint

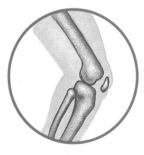

Knee

The knees are hinge joints. A hinge joint is similar to a door hinge. It allows bones to move back and forth in one direction.

The joint between the skull and neck is a pivot joint. It allows the head to move up and down, and side to side.

Pivot joint

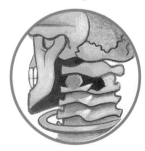

Neck

The Muscular System

1 A message from your brain causes this muscle, called the biceps, to contract. When a muscle contracts, it becomes shorter and thicker. As the biceps contracts, it pulls on the arm bone it is attached to.

2 Most muscles work in pairs to move bones. This muscle, called the triceps, relaxes when the biceps contracts. When a muscle relaxes, it becomes longer and thinner.

3 To straighten your arm, a message from your brain causes the triceps to contract. When the triceps contracts, it pulls on the bone it is attached to.

4 As the triceps contracts, the biceps relaxes. Your arm straightens.

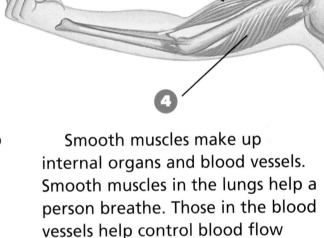

Three types of muscles make up the body—skeletal muscle, cardiac muscle, and smooth muscle.

The muscles that are attached to and move bones are called skeletal muscles. These muscles are attached to bones by a tough cord called a tendon. Skeletal muscles pull bones to move them. Muscles do not push bones.

Cardiac muscles are found in only one place in the body—the heart. The walls of the heart are made of strong cardiac muscles. When cardiac muscles contract, they squeeze blood out of the heart. When cardiac muscles relax, the heart fills with more blood.

Smooth muscles make up internal organs and blood vessels. Smooth muscles in the lungs help a person breathe. Those in the blood vessels help control blood flow around the body.

CARE!

- **Exercise to strengthen your muscles.**
- **Eat the right foods.**
- **Get plenty of rest.**

The Circulatory System

The circulatory system consists of the heart, blood vessels, and blood. Circulation is the flow of blood through the body. Blood is a liquid that contains red blood cells, white blood cells, and platelets. Red blood cells carry oxygen and nutrients to cells. White blood cells work to fight germs that enter the body. Platelets are cell fragments that make the blood clot.

The heart is a muscular organ about the size of a fist. It beats about 70 to 90 times a minute, pumping blood through the blood vessels. Arteries carry blood away from the heart. Some arteries carry blood to the lungs, where the cells pick up oxygen. Other arteries carry oxygen-rich blood from the lungs to all other parts of the body. Veins carry blood from other parts of the body back to the heart. Blood in most veins carries the wastes released by cells and has little oxygen. Blood flows from arteries to veins through narrow vessels called capillaries.

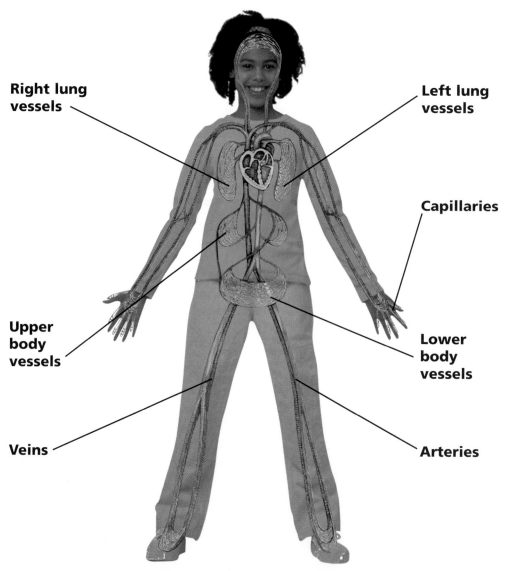

Right lung vessels

Left lung vessels

Capillaries

Upper body vessels

Lower body vessels

Veins

Arteries

The Heart

The heart has two sides, right and left, separated by a thick muscular wall. Each side has two chambers for blood. The upper chamber is the atrium. The lower chamber is the ventricle. Blood enters the heart through the vena cava. It leaves the heart through the aorta.

The pulmonary artery carries blood from the body into the lungs. Here carbon dioxide leaves the blood to be exhaled by the lungs. Fresh oxygen enters the blood to be carried to every cell in the body. Blood returns from the lungs to the heart through the pulmonary veins.

CARE!

- **Don't smoke. The nicotine in tobacco makes the heart beat faster and work harder to pump blood.**

- **Never take illegal drugs, such as cocaine or heroin. They can damage the heart and cause heart failure.**

How the Heart Works

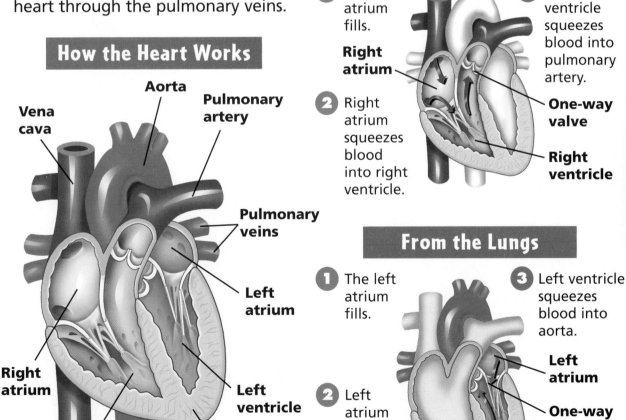

Vena cava

Aorta

Pulmonary artery

Pulmonary veins

Left atrium

Left ventricle

Right atrium

Right ventricle

Muscle wall

To the Lungs

1 The right atrium fills.

Right atrium

2 Right atrium squeezes blood into right ventricle.

3 Right ventricle squeezes blood into pulmonary artery.

One-way valve

Right ventricle

From the Lungs

1 The left atrium fills.

2 Left atrium squeezes blood into left ventricle.

3 Left ventricle squeezes blood into aorta.

Left atrium

One-way valve

Left ventricle

R 25

The Respiratory System

The process of getting and using oxygen in the body is called respiration. When a person inhales, air is pulled into the nose or mouth. The air travels down into the trachea. In the chest the trachea divides into two bronchial tubes. One bronchial tube enters each lung. Each bronchial tube branches into smaller tubes called bronchioles.

At the end of each bronchiole are tiny air sacs called alveoli. The alveoli exchange carbon dioxide for oxygen.

Oxygen comes from the air we breathe. Two muscles control breathing, the lungs and a dome-shaped sheet of muscle called the diaphragm.

To inhale, the diaphragm contracts and pulls down. To exhale, the diaphragm relaxes and returns to its dome shape.

CARE!

- **Don't smoke. Smoking damages your respiratory system.**

- **Exercise to strengthen your breathing muscles.**

- **If you ever have trouble breathing, tell an adult at once.**

Air Flow

Carbon dioxide | Oxygen

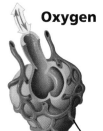

Carbon dioxide diffuses into the alveoli. From there it is exhaled.

Capillary net

Throat

Trachea

Alveoli

Fresh oxygen diffuses from the alveoli to the blood.

Lungs

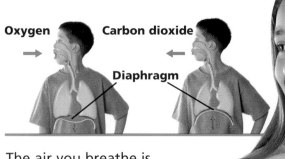

Oxygen →   Carbon dioxide ←

Diaphragm

The air you breathe is about 21 percent oxygen.

The blood in the capillaries of your lungs has very little oxygen.

The blood has a higher concentration of carbon dioxide than air.

Activity Pyramid

Physical fitness is the condition in which the body is healthy and works the best it can. It involves working the skeletal muscles, bones, joints, heart, and respiratory system.

Occasionally
Inactive pastimes such as watching TV, playing board games, talking on the phone

2–3 times a week
Leisure activities such as gardening, golf, softball

3–5 times a week
Aerobic activities such as swimming, biking, climbing; sports activities such as basketball, handball

The activity pyramid shows you the kinds of exercises and other activities you should be doing to make your body more physically fit.

Daily Substitute activity for inactivity—take the stairs, walk instead of riding, bike instead of taking the bus

Food Guide Pyramid

To make sure the body stays fit and healthy, a person needs to eat a balanced diet. The Food Guide Pyramid shows how many servings of each group a person should eat every day.

CARE!

- Stay active every day.
- Eat a balanced diet.
- Drink plenty of water—6 to 8 large glasses a day.

Fats, oils, and sweets
Use sparingly

Milk, yogurt, and cheese group
2–3 servings

Meat, dry beans, eggs, and nuts group
2–3 servings

Vegetable group
3–5 servings

Fruit group
2–4 servings

Bread, cereal, rice, and pasta group
6–11 servings

The Digestive System

Digestion is the process of breaking down food into simple substances the body can use. Digestion begins when a person chews food. Chewing breaks the food down into smaller pieces and moistens it with saliva. Saliva is produced by the salivary glands.

Digested food is absorbed in the small intestine. The walls of the small intestine are lined with villi. Villi are tiny fingerlike projections that absorb digested food. From the villi the blood transports nutrients to every part of the body.

CARE!

- Chew your food well.
- Drink plenty of water to help move food through your digestive system.

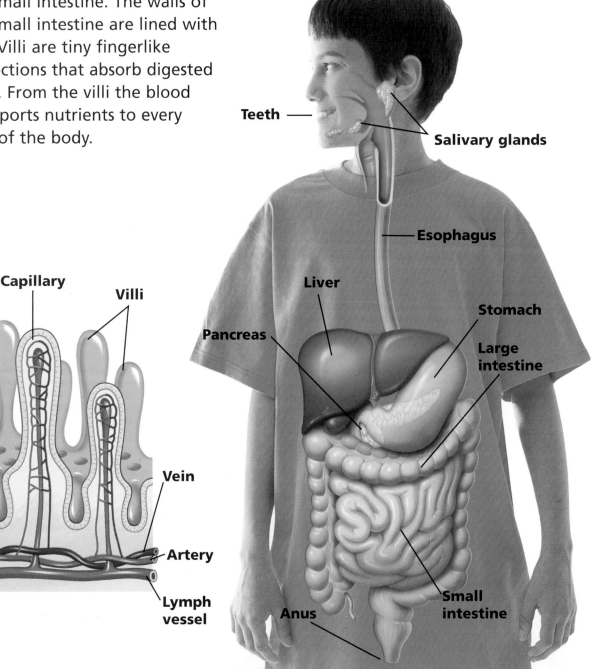

Teeth

Salivary glands

Esophagus

Liver

Stomach

Pancreas

Large intestine

Capillary

Villi

Vein

Artery

Lymph vessel

Anus

Small intestine

The Excretory System

Excretion is the process of removing waste products from the body. The liver filters wastes from the blood and converts them into urea. Urea is then carried to the kidneys for excretion.

The skin takes part in excretion when a person sweats. Glands in the inner layer of the skin produce sweat. Sweat is mostly water. Sweat tastes salty because it contains mineral salts the body doesn't need. There is also a tiny amount of urea in sweat.

Sweat is excreted onto the outer layer of the skin. Evaporation into the air takes place in part because of body heat. When sweat evaporates, a person feels cooler.

How You Sweat

Glands under your skin push sweat up to the surface, where it collects.

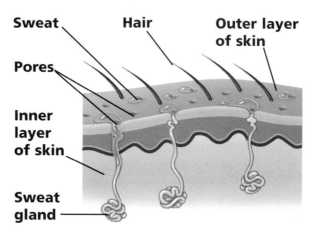

Sweat — Hair — Outer layer of skin — Pores — Inner layer of skin — Sweat gland

CARE!

- Wash regularly to avoid body odor, clogged pores, and skin irritation.

How Your Kidneys Work

1. Blood enters the kidney through an artery and flows into capillaries.

2. Sugars, salts, water, urea, and other wastes move from the capillaries to tiny nephrons.

3. Nutrients return to the blood and flow back out through veins.

4. Urea and other wastes become urine, which flows down the ureters.

5. Urine is stored in the bladder and excreted through the urethra.

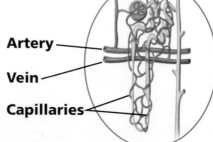

Artery — Vein — Capillaries

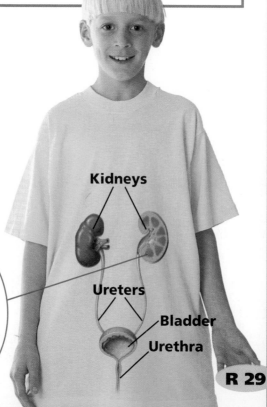

Kidneys — Ureters — Bladder — Urethra

The Nervous System

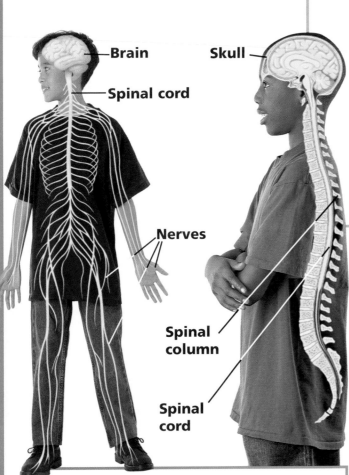

Brain
Spinal cord
Skull
Nerves
Spinal column
Spinal cord

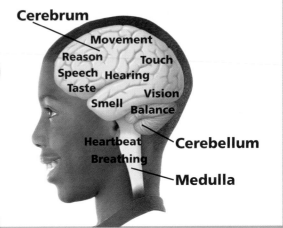

Cerebrum
Movement
Reason
Touch
Speech Hearing
Taste
Vision
Smell
Balance
Heartbeat
Breathing
Cerebellum
Medulla

CARE!

- To protect the brain and spinal cord, wear protective headgear when you play sports or exercise.

- Stay away from alcohol, which is a depressant and slows down the nervous system.

- Stay away from drugs, such as stimulants, which can speed up the nervous system.

The nervous system has two parts. The brain and the spinal cord are the central nervous system. All other nerves are the outer nervous system.

The largest part of the brain is the cerebrum. A deep groove separates the right half, or hemisphere, of the cerebrum from the left half. Both sides of the cerebrum contain control centers for the senses.

The cerebellum lies below the cerebrum. It coordinates the skeletal muscles. It also helps in keeping balance.

The brain stem connects to the spinal cord. The lowest part of the brain stem is the medulla. It controls heartbeat, breathing, blood pressure, and the muscles in the digestive system.

The Endocrine System

Hormones are chemicals that control body functions. A gland that produces hormones is called an endocrine gland. Sweat from sweat glands flows out of tubes called ducts. Endocrine glands have no ducts.

The endocrine glands are scattered around the body. Each gland makes one or more hormones. Every hormone seeks out a target organ. This is the place in the body where the hormone acts.

Some Glands in the Endocrine System

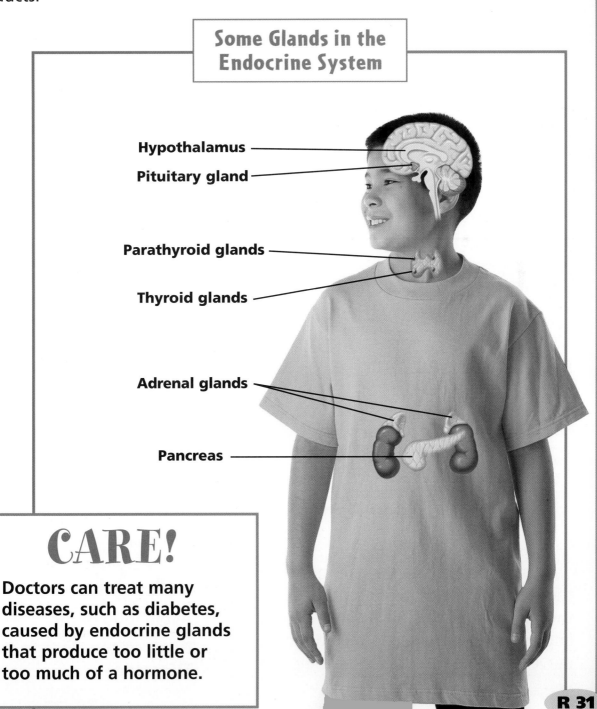

Hypothalamus

Pituitary gland

Parathyroid glands

Thyroid glands

Adrenal glands

Pancreas

CARE!

- Doctors can treat many diseases, such as diabetes, caused by endocrine glands that produce too little or too much of a hormone.

The Senses

Seeing

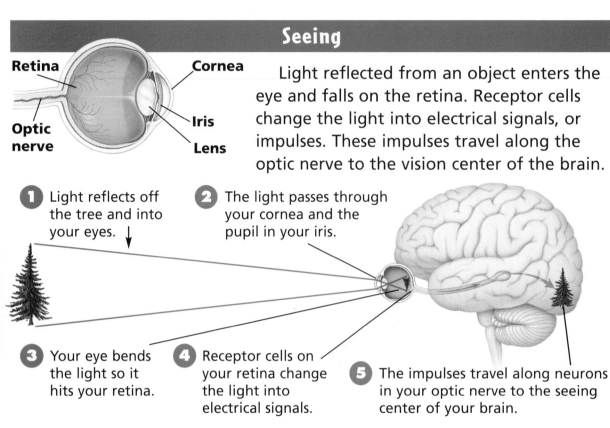

Retina **Cornea**

Optic nerve **Iris** **Lens**

Light reflected from an object enters the eye and falls on the retina. Receptor cells change the light into electrical signals, or impulses. These impulses travel along the optic nerve to the vision center of the brain.

1 Light reflects off the tree and into your eyes.

2 The light passes through your cornea and the pupil in your iris.

3 Your eye bends the light so it hits your retina.

4 Receptor cells on your retina change the light into electrical signals.

5 The impulses travel along neurons in your optic nerve to the seeing center of your brain.

Hearing

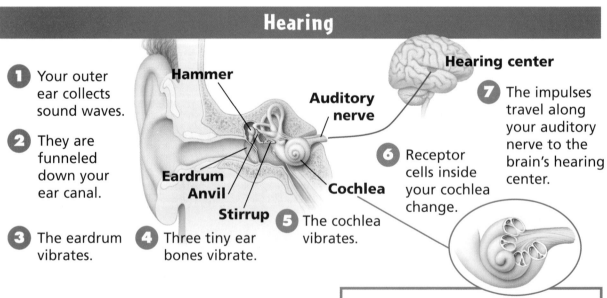

Hammer

Auditory nerve

Hearing center

Eardrum
Anvil

Stirrup

Cochlea

1 Your outer ear collects sound waves.

2 They are funneled down your ear canal.

3 The eardrum vibrates.

4 Three tiny ear bones vibrate.

5 The cochlea vibrates.

6 Receptor cells inside your cochlea change.

7 The impulses travel along your auditory nerve to the brain's hearing center.

Sound waves enter the ear and cause the eardrum to vibrate. Receptor cells in the ear change the sound waves into impulses that travel along the auditory nerve to the hearing center of the brain.

CARE!

- **Avoid loud music.**
- **Don't sit too close to the TV screen.**

The Senses

Smelling

The sense of smell is really the ability to detect chemicals in the air. When a person breathes, chemicals dissolve in mucus in the upper part of the nose. When the chemicals come in contact with receptor cells, the cells send impulses along the olfactory nerve to the smelling center of the brain.

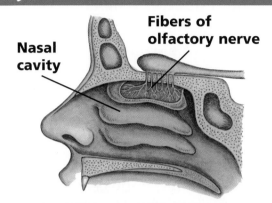

Nasal cavity

Fibers of olfactory nerve

Tasting

When a person eats, chemicals in food dissolve in saliva. Inside each taste bud are receptors that can sense the four main tastes—sweet, sour, salty, and bitter. The receptors send impulses along a nerve to the taste center of the brain. The brain identifies the taste of the food.

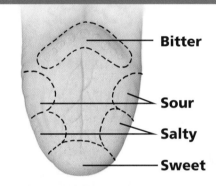

Bitter

Sour

Salty

Sweet

Touching

Receptor cells in the skin help a person tell hot from cold, wet from dry, and the light touch of a feather from the pressure of stepping on a stone. Each receptor cell sends impulses along sensory nerves to the spinal cord. The spinal cord then sends the impulses to the touch center of the brain.

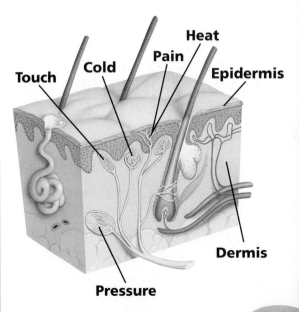

Touch   Cold   Pain   Heat   Epidermis

Dermis

Pressure

CARE!

- To prevent the spread of germs, always cover your mouth and nose when you cough or sneeze.

The Immune System

The immune system helps the body fight disease. When a person has a cut, germ-fighting white blood cells rush to the wound. There are white blood cells in the blood vessels and in the lymph vessels. Lymph vessels are similar to blood vessels. Instead of blood, they carry lymph. Lymph is a straw-colored fluid surrounding body cells.

Lymph nodes filter out harmful materials in the body. They also produce white blood cells to fight infections. Swollen lymph nodes in the neck are a clue that the body is fighting germs.

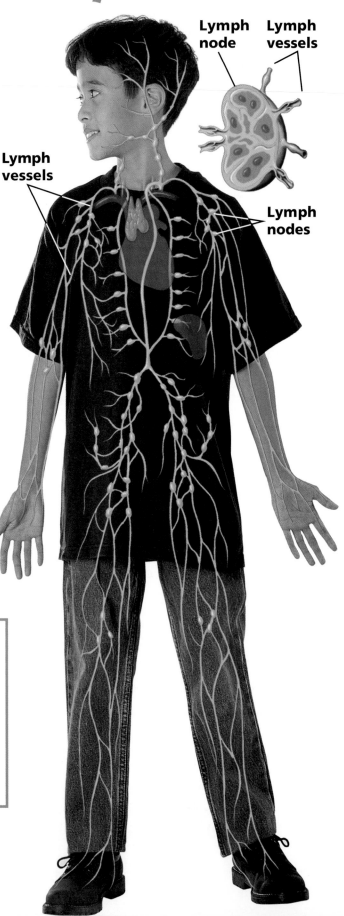

Lymph node

Lymph vessels

Lymph vessels

Lymph nodes

Lymph vessels run through your body to collect fluid and return it to the bloodstream.

CARE!

- **Be sure to get immunized against common diseases.**
- **Keep cuts clean to prevent infection.**

Glossary

This Glossary will help you to pronounce and understand the meanings of the Science Words introduced in this book. The page number at the end of the definition tells where the word appears.

A

adaptation (ad'əp tā'shən) A special characteristic that helps an organism survive. (p. B50)

air (âr) A mixture of gases and dust. (p. D6)

air pressure (âr presh'ər) The force of air pushing down on Earth. (p. D9)

algae (al'jē) *pl. n., sing.* (-gə) Tiny one-celled organisms. (pp. B9, B27)

amber (am'bər) Hardened tree sap, often a source of insect fossils. (p. C22)

amphibian (am fib'ē ən) An animal that spends part of its life in water and part of its life on land. (p. A72)

anemometer (an'ə mom'i tər) A device that measures wind speed. (p. D25)

aqueduct (ak'wə dukt') A pipe or channel for carrying water over long distances. (p. C32)

atmosphere (at'məs fîr') Gases that surround Earth. (p. D6)

atom (at'əm) The smallest particle of matter. (p. F28)

axis (ak'sis) A real or imaginary line through the center of a spinning object. (p. D37)

PRONUNCIATION KEY

The following symbols are used throughout the McGraw-Hill Science 2002 Glossaries.

a	at	e	end	o	hot	u	up	hw	white	ə	about
ā	ape	ē	me	ō	old	ū	use	ng	song		taken
ä	far	i	it	ôr	fork	ü	rule	th	thin		pencil
âr	care	ī	ice	oi	oil	ù	pull	th	this		lemon
ô	law	îr	pierce	ou	out	ûr	turn	zh	measure		circus

′ = primary accent; shows which syllable takes the main stress, such as **kil** in **kilogram** (kil'ə gram').
′ = secondary accent; shows which syllables take lighter stresses, such as **gram** in **kilogram.**

bacteria, (bak tîr′ē ə) One-celled living things. (p. B18)

barometer (bə rom′i tər) A device for measuring air pressure. (p. D24)

bird (bûrd) An animal that has a beak, feathers, two wings, and two legs. (p. A73)

bulb (bulb) The underground stem of such plants as onions and irises. (p. A30)

C

camouflage (kam′ə fläzh) An adaptation that allows animals to blend into their surroundings. (p. B52)

carbon dioxide and oxygen cycles (kär′bən dī ok′sīd and ok′sə jən sī′kəlz) The process of passing oxygen and carbon dioxide from one population to another in both water and land habitats. (p. B27)

carnivore (kär′nə vôr′) An animal that eats only other animals. (p. B20)

cast (kast) A fossil formed or shaped inside a mold. (p. C23)

cell (sel) **1.** The basic building block of life. (p. A10) **2.** A source of electricity. (p. F72)

cell membrane (sel mem′brān′) The thin outer covering of a cell. (p. A10)

cell wall (sel wôl) A stiff layer outside the cell membrane of plant cells. (p. A11)

chemical change (kəm′i kəl chānj) A change that forms a different kind of matter. (p. F30)

chloroplast (klôr′ə plast′) One of the small green bodies inside a plant cell that makes foods for the plant. (p. A11)

circuit (sûr′kit) The path electricity flows through. (p. F72)

classify (klas′ə fi) To place materials that share properties together in groups. (p. S7)

communicate (kə mü′ni kāt′) To share information. (p. S7)

community (kə mü′ni tē) All the living things in an ecosystem. (p. B6)

competition (kom′pi tish′ən) The struggle among organisms for water, food, or other needs. (p. B42)

compound (kom′pound) Two or more elements put together. (p. F30)

compound machine (kom′pound mə shēn′) Two or more simple machines put together. (p. E57)

condense (kən dens′) *v.* To change from a gas to a liquid. (pp. C31, F17) —**condensation** (kon′den sā′shən) *n.* (p. D17)

conductor (kən duk′tər) A material that heat travels through easily. (p. F46)

conifer (kon′ə fər) A tree that produces seeds inside of cones. (p. A28)

conserve (kən sûrv′) To save, protect, or use something wisely without wasting it. (p. C34)

consumer (kən sü′mər) An organism that eats producers or other consumers. (pp. A40, B17)

crater (krā′tər) A hollow area in the ground. (p. D49)

cutting (kut′ing) A plant part from which a new plant can grow. (p. A30)

cytoplasm (sī′tə pla′zəm) A clear, jellylike material that fills both plant and animal cells. (p. A10)

D

decibel (dB) (des′ə bel′) A unit that measures loudness. (p. F69)

decomposer (dē′kəm pō′zər) An organism that breaks down dead plant and animal material. *Decomposers* recycle chemicals so they can be used again. (p. B18)

define based on observations (di fīn′ bāst ôn ob′zər vā′shənz) To put together a description that relies on examination and experience. (p. S7)

degree (di grē′) The unit of measurement for temperature. (p. F43)

PRONUNCIATION KEY

a at; ā ape; ä far; âr care; ô law; e end; ē me; i it; ī ice; îr pierce; o hot; ō old; ôr fork; oi oil; ou out; u up; ū use; ü rule; u̇ pull; ûr turn; hw white; ng song; th thin; <u>th</u> this; zh measure; ə about, taken, pencil, lemon, circus

desert (dez′ərt) A hot dry place with very little rain. (p. B55)

development (di vel′əp mənt) The way a living thing changes during its life. (p. A6)

distance (dis′təns) The length between two places. (p. E7)

E

earthquake (ûrth′kwāk) A sudden movement in the rocks that make up Earth's crust. (p. C72)

ecosystem (ek′ō sis′təm) All the living and nonliving things in an environment and all their interactions. (p. B6)

electric current (i lek′trik kûr′ənt) Electricity that flows through a circuit. (p. F72)

element (el′ə mənt) A building block of matter. (p. F28)

embryo (em′brē ō) A young organism that is just beginning to grow. (p. A26)

endangered (en dān′jərd) Close to becoming extinct; having very few of its kind left. (p. B64)

energy (en′ər jē) The ability to do work. (pp. A18, E39)

energy pyramid (en′ər jē pir′ə mid′) A diagram that shows how energy is used in an ecosystem. (p. B22)

environment (en vī′rən mənt) The things that make up an area, such as land, water, and air. (p. A8)

erosion (i rō′zhən) The carrying away of weathered materials. (p. C62)

evaporate (i vap′ə rāt′) v. To change from a liquid to a gas. (pp. C31, F17) —**evaporation** (i vap′ə rā′shən′) n. (p. D17)

experiment (ek sper′ə ment′) To perform a test to support or disprove a hypothesis. (p. S7)

extinct (ek stingkt) Died out, leaving no more of that type of organism alive. (p. B66)

F

fertilizer (fûr′tə lī′z) A substance added to the soil that is used to make plants grow. (p. C42)

first quarter (fûrst kwôr′tər) A phase of the Moon in which the right half is visible and growing larger. (p. D47)

fish (fish) An animal that lives its whole life in water. (p. A71)

flood (flud) A great rush of water over usually dry land. (p. C71)

flowering plant (flou'ər ing plant) A plant that produces seeds inside of flowers. (p. A28)

food chain (füd chān) A series of organisms that depend on one another for food. (p. B17)

food web (füd web) Several food chains that are connected. (p. B20)

force (fôrs) A push or pull, such as the one that moves a lever. (pp. E14, E44)

form a hypothesis (fôrm ə hī poth'ə sis) To make a statement that can be tested in answer to a question. (p. S7)

fossil (fos'əl) The imprint or remains of something that lived long ago. (p. C22)

freeze (frēz) To turn from water to ice. (p. F17)

friction (frik'shən) A force that occurs when one object rubs against another. (p. E26)

fuel (fū'əl) A substance burned for its energy. (p. C26)

fulcrum (fūl'krəm) The point where a lever turns or pivots. (p. E44)

full Moon (fūl mün) or **second quarter** (sek'ənd kwôr'tər) The phase of the Moon in which all of its sunlit half is visible from Earth. (p. D47)

fungi, (fun'jī) *pl. n., sing.* **fungus** (fung'gəs) One- or many-celled organisms that absorb food from dead organisms. (p. B18)

G

gas (gas) Matter that has no definite shape or volume. (p. F14)

germinate (jûr'mə nāt) To begin to grow, as when the right conditions allow a seed to develop. (p. A26)

PRONUNCIATION KEY

a at; ā ape; ä far; âr care; ô law; e end; ē me; i it; ī ice; îr pierce; o hot; ō old; ôr fork; oi oil; ou out; u up; ū use; ü rule; u̇ pull; ûr turn; hw white; ng song; th thin; th this; zh measure; ə about, taken, pencil, lemon, circus

glacier (glā′shər) A large mass of ice in motion. (p. C62)

gram (gram) A metric unit used to measure mass; 1,000 *grams* equals 1 kilogram. (p. F9)

gravity (grav′i tē) A pulling force between two objects, such as Earth and you. (p. E16)

groundwater (ground wô′tər) Water stored in the cracks of underground rocks and soil. (p. C33)

H

habitat (hab′i tat) The home of a living thing. (p. B7)

heat (hēt) A form of energy that makes things warmer. (p. F42)

herbivore (hûr′bə vôr′) An animal that eats only plants. (p. B20)

heredity (hə red′i tē) The passing of traits from parents to offspring. (p. A27)

hibernate (hī′bər nāt′) To rest or sleep through the cold winter. (p. A46)

host (hōst). An organism that a parasite lives with. (p. B31)

humus (hü′məs) Leftover decomposed plant and animal matter. (p. C14)

hurricane (hûr′i kān′) A violent storm with strong winds and heavy rains. (p. C70)

I

igneous rock (ig′nē əs rok) A "fire-made" rock formed from melted rock material. (p. C8)

imprint (im′print′) A shallow mark or print in a rock. (p. C23)

inclined plane (in klīnd′ plān) A flat surface that is raised at one end. (p. E54)

infer (in fûr′) To form an idea from facts or observations. (p. S7)

inherited trait (in her′i təd trāt) A characteristic that comes from your parents. (p. A56)

inner planet (in′ər plan′it) Any of the four planets in the solar system that are closest to the Sun: Mercury, Venus, Earth, and Mars. (p. D56)

insulator (in′sə lā′tər) A material that heat doesn't travel through easily. (p. F46)

interpret data (in tûr′prit dā′tə) To use the information that has been gathered to answer questions or solve a problem. (p. S7)

K

key (kē) A table that shows what different symbols on a map stand for. (p. E10)

kilogram (kil′ə gram′) A metric unit used to measure mass; 1 *kilogram* equals 1,000 grams. (p. F9)

L

landform (land′fôrm′) A feature on Earth's surface. (p. C54)

last quarter (last kwôr′tər) or **third quarter** (thûrd kwôr′tər) The phase of the waning Moon in which the left half is visible but growing smaller. (p. D47)

leaf (lēf) A plant part that grows from the stem and helps the plant get air and make food. (p. A18)

learned trait (lûrnd trāt) Something that you are taught or learn from experience. (p. A56)

lens (lenz) A curved piece of glass. (p. D58)

lever (lev′ər) A straight bar that moves on a fixed point. (p. E44)

life cycle (līf sī′kəl) All the stages in an organism's life. (p. A26)

liquid (lik′wid) Matter that has a definite volume but not a definite shape. (p. F14)

liter (lē′tər) A metric unit used to measure volume. (p. F9)

load (lōd) The object that a lever lifts or moves. (p. E44)

loam (lōm) A kind of soil that contains clay, sand, silt, and humus. Plants grow well in loam. (p. C15)

luster (lus′tər) How an object reflects light. (p. F6)

PRONUNCIATION KEY

a at; ā ape; ä far; âr care; ô law; e end; ē me; i it; ī ice; îr pierce; o hot; ō old; ôr fork; oi oil; ou out; u up; ū use; ü rule; u̇ pull; ûr turn; hw white; ng song; th thin; th this; zh measure; ə about, taken, pencil, lemon, circus

machine (mə shēn′) A tool that makes work easier to do. (p. E44)

magnetism (mag′ni tiz′əm) The property of an object that makes it attract iron. (p. F26)

make a model (māk ə mod′əl) To make something to represent an object or event. (p. S7)

mammal (mam′əl) An animal with fur that feeds its young with milk. (p. A74)

map (map) A flat drawing that shows the positions of things. (p. E10)

mass (mas) The amount of matter in an object. (p. F7)

matter (mat′ər) Anything that takes up space and has mass. (pp. D16, F6)

measure (mezh′ər) To find the size, volume, area, mass, weight, or temperature of an object, or how long an event occurs. (p. S7)

melt (melt) To change from a solid to a liquid. (p. F17)

metal (met′əl) A shiny material found in the ground. (p. F26)

metamorphic rock (met′ə môr′fik rok) A rock that has changed form through squeezing and heating. (p. C9)

metamorphosis (met′ə môr′fə sis) A change in the body form of an organism. (p. A52)

microscope (mī′krə skōp′) A device that uses glass lenses to allow people to see very small things. (p. A10)

migrate (mī′grāt) To move to another place. (p. A46)

mimicry (mim′i krē) The imitation by one animal of the traits of another. (p. B53)

mineral (min′ə rəl) A naturally occurring substance, neither plant nor animal. (pp. A16, C6)

mixture (miks′chər) Different types of matter mixed together. The properties of each kind of matter in the mixture does not change. (p. F18)

mold (mold) An empty space in a rock that once contained an object such as a dead organism. (p. C23)

motion (mō′shən) A change in position. (p. E8)

mountain (moun'tən) The highest of Earth's landforms. *Mountains* often have steep sides and pointed tops. (p. C55)

N

natural resource (nach'ər əl rē'sôrs') A material on Earth that is necessary or useful to people. (p. C38)

nectar (nek'tər) The sugary liquid in flowers that lures insects that aid in pollination. (p. A28)

new Moon (nü mün) A phase of the Moon in which none of its sunlit half is visible from Earth. (p. D47)

newton (nü'tən) The unit used to measure pushes and pulls. (pp. E17, F10)

niche (nich) The job or role an organism has in an ecosystem. (p. B44)

nonrenewable resource (non'ri nü'ə bəl rē'sôrs') A resource that cannot be reused or replaced easily. (p. C41)

nucleus (nü'klē əs) The control center of a cell. (p. A11)

O

observe (əb sûrv') To use one or more of the senses to identify or learn about an object or event. (p. S7)

omnivore (om'nə vôr') An animal that eats both plants and animals. (p. B21)

opaque (ō pāk') A material that doesn't allow light to pass through. (p. F54)

orbit (ôr'bit) The path an object follows as it revolves around another object. (p. D38)

organ (ôr'gən) A group of tissues that work together. (p. A62)

PRONUNCIATION KEY

a at; ā ape; ä far; âr care; ô law; e end; ē me; i it; ī ice; îr pierce; o hot; ō old; ôr fork; oi oil; ou out; u up; ū use; ü rule; u̇ pull; ûr turn; hw white; ng song; th thin; <u>th</u> this; zh measure; ə about, taken, pencil, lemon, circus

organism (ôr'gə niz'əm) Any living thing. (p. A6)

outer planet (out'ər plan'it) Any of the five planets in the solar system that are farthest from the Sun: Jupiter, Saturn, Uranus, Neptune, and Pluto. (p. D56)

oxygen (ok'sə jən) A gas that is in air and water. (p. A19)

P

parasite (par'ə sīt'). An organism that lives in or on a host. (p. B31)

perish (per'ish) To fail to survive. (p. B63)

phase (fāz) An apparent change in the Moon's shape. (p. D46)

physical change (fiz'i kəl chānj) A change in the way matter looks that leaves the matter itself unchanged. (p. F16)

pitch (pich) How high or low a sound is. (p. F66)

plain (plān) Wide flat lands. (p. C55)

planet (plan'it) Any of the nine large bodies that orbit the Sun. In order from the Sun outward, they are Mercury, Venus, Earth, Mars, Jupiter, Saturn, Uranus, Neptune, and Pluto. (p. D54)

pollen (pol'ən) A powdery material needed by the eggs of flowers to make seeds. (p. A28)

pollution (pə lü'shən) The adding of harmful substances to the water, air, or land. (p. C42)

population (pop'yə lā'shən) All the members of a single type of organism in an ecosystem. (p. B6)

position (pə zish'ən) The location of an object. (p. E6)

precipitation (pri sip'i tā'shən) Water in the atmosphere that falls to Earth as rain, snow, hail, or sleet. (p. D19)

predator (pred'ə tər) An animal that hunts for food. (p. B28)

predict (pri dikt') To state possible results of an event or experiment. (p. S7)

prey (prā) The animals that predators eat. (p. B28)

prism (pri′zəm) A thick piece of glass that refracts light. (p. F57)

producer (prə dü′sər) An organism such as a plant that makes its own food. (p. B16)

property (prop′ər tē) Any characteristic of matter that you can observe. (p. F6)

pulley (pul′ē) A simple machine that uses a wheel and a rope. (p. E48)

R

rain gauge (rān gāj) A device that measures how much precipitation has fallen. (p. D24)

ramp (ramp) Another name for an inclined plane. (p. E54)

recycle (rē sī′kəl) To treat something so it can be used again. (p. C44)

reduce (ri düs′) To use less of something. (p. C44)

reflect (ri flekt′) The bouncing of light off a surface. (p. F55)

refract (ri frakt′) The bending of light as it passes through matter. (p. F56)

relocate (rē lō′kāt) To find a new home. (p. B63)

renewable resource (ri nü′ə bəl rē′sôrs′) A resource that can be replaced or used over and over again. (p. C40)

reproduction (rē′prə duk′shən) The way organisms make more of their own kind. (p. A7)

reptile (rep′təl′) An animal that lives on land and has waterproof skin. (p. A72)

reservoir (rez′ər vwär′) A storage area for fresh water supplies. (p. C32)

respond (ri spond′) To react to changes in the environment. (p. A8)

reuse (rē ūz′) v. To use something again. (p. C44)

revolve (ri volv′) To move around another object. (p. D38)

PRONUNCIATION KEY

a at; ā ape; ä far; âr care; ô law; e end; ē me; i it; ī ice; îr pierce; o hot; ō old; ôr fork; oi oil; ou out; u up; ū use; ü rule; u̇ pull; ûr turn; hw white; ng song; th thin; th this; zh measure; ə about, taken, pencil, lemon, circus

river (riv′ər) A large stream of water that flows across the land. (p. C55)

root (rüt) A plant part that takes in water and grows under the ground. (p. A17)

rotate (rō′tāt) To turn around. (p. D36)

S

sand dune (sand dün) A mound of windblown sand. (p. C55)

sapling (sap′ling) A very young tree. (p. A6)

satellite (sat′ə līt′) Any object that orbits another larger body in space. (p. D46)

scavenger (skav′ən jər) An animal that gets its food by eating dead organisms. (p. B29)

screw (skrü) An inclined plane wrapped into a spiral. (p. E56)

sedimentary rock (sed′ə men′tə rē rok) A kind of rock formed when sand, mud, pebbles at the bottom of rivers, lakes, and oceans pile up. (p. C8)

seedling (sēd′ling) A young plant. (p. A27)

shelter (shel′tər) A place or object that protects an animal and keeps It safe. (p. A44)

silt (silt) Soil that is made of tiny rocks. *Silt* is carried by water and deposited as sediment. (p. C14)

simple machine (sim′pəl mə shēn′) A machine with few or no moving parts. (p. E44)

soil (soil) A mixture of tiny rock particles, minerals, and decayed plant and animal materials. (p. C14)

solar system (sō′lər sis′təm) The Sun and all the objects that orbit the Sun. (p. D54)

solid (sol′id) Matter that has a definite shape and volume. (p. F14)

solution (sə lü′shən) A kind of mixture in which one or more types of matter are mixed evenly in another kind of matter. (p. F19)

speed (spēd) How fast an object moves over a certain distance. (p. E9)

sphere (sfîr) A body that has the shape of a ball or globe. (p. D36)

spore (spôr) One of the tiny reproductive bodies of ferns and mosses, similar to the seeds of other plants. (p. A30)

star (stär) A huge, hot sphere of gases, like the Sun, that gives off its own light. (p. D55)

stem (stem) A plant part that supports the plant. (p. A17)

switch (swich) A lever that opens or closes an electric circuit. (p. F73)

system (sis'təm) A group of parts that work together. (p. A62)

texture (teks'chər) How the surface of an object feels to the touch. (p. F6)

thermometer (thər mom'ə tər) An instrument used to measure temperature. (pp. D8, D24)

tissue (tish'ü) A group of cells that are alike. (p. A62)

tornado (tôr nā'dō) A violent, whirling wind that moves across the ground in a narrow path. (p. C70)

tuber (tü'bər) The underground stem of a plant such as the potato. (p. A30)

tundra (tun'drə) A cold dry place. (p. B55)

telescope (tel'ə skōp') A tool that gathers light to make faraway objects appear closer. (p. D58)

temperature (tem'pər ə cher) How hot or cold something is. (pp. D8, F43)

use numbers (ūz num'bərz) To order, count, add, subtract, multiply, and divide to explain data. (p. S7)

use variables (ūz vâr'ē ə bəlz) To identify and separate things in an experiment that can be changed or controlled. (p. S7)

PRONUNCIATION KEY

a at; ā ape; ä far; âr care; ô law; e end; ē me; i it; ī ice; îr pierce; o hot; ō old; ôr fork; oi oil; ou out; u up; ū use; ü rule; ù pull; ûr turn; hw white; ng song; th thin; <u>th</u> this; zh measure; ə about, taken, pencil, lemon, circus

valley (val′ē) An area of low land lying between hills or mountains. (p. C55)

vibrate (vī′brāt) To move back and forth quickly. (p. F64)

volcano (vol kā′nō) An opening in the surface of Earth. (p. C73)

volume (vol′ūm) **1.** A measure of how much space matter takes up. (p. F7) **2.** How loud or soft a sound is. (p. F67)

water cycle (wô′tər sī′kəl) The movement of Earth's water over and over from a liquid to a gas and from a gas to a liquid. (pp. C31, D19)

water vapor (wô′tər vā′pər) Water in the form of a gas in Earth's atmosphere. (p. D17)

weather (we<u>th</u>′ər) The condition of the atmosphere at a given time and place. (p. D6)

weather vane (we<u>th</u>′ər vān) A device that indicates the direction of the wind. (p. D25)

weathering (we<u>th</u>′ər ing) The process that causes rocks to crumble, crack, and break. (p. C60)

wedge (wej) Two inclined planes placed back to back. (p. E55)

weight (wāt) The measure of the pull of gravity between an object and Earth. (p. E17)

wheel and axle (hwēl and ak′səl) A wheel that turns on a post. (p. E47)

wind (wind) Moving air. (p. D10)

windlass (wind′ləs) A wheel and axle machine that is turned by a hand crank to lift a bucket in a well. (p. E47)

work (wûrk) The force that changes the motion of an object. (p. E38)

Index

A

Adaptations, B48–49*, B50–56*, B57
Adult, A52–53
Air, A8, A42–43, A54–55, A65, B16, B26–27, B33, C38, C40, D4–5*, D6–11, D49
Air mass, D10
Air pollution, A58, C43*, C46
Air pressure, D9*, D11, D12, D24
Air temperature, D8, D20*, D24, D37
Algae, B9, B27
Allen, Christina, B70–71
Aluminum, F27
Amber, C22
Amphibians, A72
Anemometer, D25
Animals, A38–39*, A40–41*, A42–49, A50–51*, A52–57, A60–61*, A62–65, A66*, A68–69*, A70–75, B4–5*, B6–10*, B11–15*, B16–19*, B20–25*, B26–32*, B33–35, B40–44*, B45–46, B48–49*, B50–57, B59*–65*, B66–67, C25, C38
  adaptations of, B48–49*, B50–56, B57
  as consumers, B16–17, B22
  classifying and comparing, A66*, A68–69*, A70–75
  competition of, B40–41*, B42–45, B46
  defenses of, B54–55
  habitats, B8–10*
  how humans depend on, B12–13
  how populations of affect each other, B28–31
  how they grow and change, A50–51*, A52–55
  how they help plants, B6–11, B26–27, B32
  how they reproduce, A52–55, A74, B32*
  life cycle of, A50–51*, A52–55
  needs of, A38–39*, A40–41*, A42–45, A47, B24–25*, B26–27
  parts of, A60–66*
  responses of, A45–46
Appendix, A62
Aqueducts, C32, C35
Area, R2–3, R7
Art link, A13, A21, A31, A47, A57, A67, B57, C11, C35, C45, D11, D21, D27, E19, E41, F11, F21, F49, F59
Astronaut, E62–63
Astronomer, D62–63
Atmosphere, D6–9*, D10–11
  layers of, D6–7
Atom, F28
Ax, E55
Axis, D37, D38, D40*, D41
Axles, E47, E57

B

Bacteria, B18–19*, B33
Bar graph, A21, B33, B67, C27, C75, D11, D23*, E5*, E18*, E29, E49*, F11, F33, R16
Barometer, D24–25*, D27
Basalt, C8
Battery, C46–47, F71*–72
Bay, C55
Bear, A54, B55
Bengal tiger, B63
Biochemist, F78–79
Bird, A73*, A75, B7, B49*, B50
Birth, A52–53
Bladderwort, B9
Body covering, A63–65, A67, B56
Body parts, A60–61*, A62–66, A67, R20–34
Body temperature, A71, A74
Bones, A63, C24
Breath, A65
Bulbs, A30

C

Cactus, A22–23
Calculator, using, R12–13
California Condor, B64
Camouflage, B52, B56*, B57
Canyon, C55
Carbon, F29, F30
Carbon dioxide, A18, B26–27, B33, F31
Carbon dioxide cycle, B27, B33
Careers, in science, A78–79, B70–71, C78–79, D62–63, E62–63, F78–79
Carnivore, B20
Carver, George Washington, C18–19
Cast, C23

* Indicates an activity related to this topic.

Caterpillar, A51*, A52–53, A57, B53

Cells, A10–11*, A13, A62–63, A67, F72–75
body, A62
cytoplasm in, A11*
electrical, F72–75
membranes, A10, A11*
nucleus of, A11*
of living things, A10–11*, A62–63, A67
wall of, A10, A11*

Celsius scale, D8, R2, R11

Centimeter, R3, R7

Chalk, C6, C61*

Changes
caused by growth, A51*–53
chemical, C60–61*, F30–33
how organisms respond to, A8, A12*, A13, A46
in direction of force, E44
in ecosystems, B58–59*, B60–66
in energy, E40*, F48
in heat, F44–45*
in land, C36–37*, C58–59*, C60–65, C68–69*, C70–75
in living things, A6–9, A12*, A13, A51*, A52–53
in matter, F16–17, F44–45*
in moon's shape, D45*–47
in motion, E23*, E24–28*
in rocks, C59*
in seasons, A46
in sound, F66, F69
in temperature, A46, C60
of position, E8
physical, F16, F21, F32–33

Chappelle, Emmett, F78–79

Charts, reading and making, A56*, A67, B5, B8, B15*, B49*, B62, C7*, C9, C44, D8, E37*, F6, F17, F69, R18–19

Chawla, Dr. Kalpana, E62–63

Chemical change, C60–61*, F30–31*

Chemicals, B18, C60–61*, F30–31*

Chicken, A55

Chlorine, F30

Chlorophyll, A18–19*

Chloroplasts, A10–11*, A19*

Circuits, electrical, F72–73*, F75

Circulatory system, R24–25

Classifying, A51, A56*, A66, A68–69*, A70–75, B10*, B15*, B17, C5*, C53*, E37*, F13*–14, F25*, F53*

Closed circuit, F73*

Clouds, C31

Coal, B46, C26–27, C38, C41

Coast, C55–56

Cold-blooded animals, A71–72

Communicating, A51*, A56*, A66*, A69*, B44*, C7*, D5*, D23*, D45*, D50*, E23*, E43*, F13*, F20*, F33*, F45*, F58*

Communication, of living things, A9

Community, B6–10*, B11

Competition, B40–41*, B42–44*, B45, B46

Compound machines, E57, E59

Compounds, F30–31, F33

Computer, using, R14–15. See also Technology link.

Condensation, C31, D17, D18, D21, F17

Conductors, F46–47, F49

Cones, A29

Conifers, A28–29, A31

Conservation, B47, C34*, C35, C44–45

Constellations, D42–43

Consumers, A40, B16–17, B19*, B21–23

Contour farming, C66

Contraction, F44–45*

Controlling an experiment, F58*

Controlling electrical flow, F73

Controlling friction, E28

Controlling heat flow, F46

Copper, F27, F28

Cover crops, C66

Craters, D49

Creosote bush, A22–23

Critical thinking, A13, A21, A31, A47, A57, A67, A75, B11, B23, B33, B45, B57, B67, C11, C17, C27, C35, C45, C57, C65, C75, D11, D21, D41, D51, D59, E11, E19, E29, E41, E49, E59, F11, F21, F33, F49, F59, F69, F75

Crop rotation, C18–19

Cuttings, A30

Cytoplasm, A10–11*

D

Dallmeier, Dr. Francisco, A78–79

Dams, C32, C35

Data, interpreting and organizing, A11*, A15*, A41*, A66*, C71*, C75, D5*, E5*, E18*, E19, F71, R19

Day, D34–35*, D36–37, 41

Death, A27*, A52

Decibel, F69

Decomposers, B18–19*, B23, B33

Degrees, F43

Desert, A22, A44, B16, B55, C52

Development, A6, A26–A29, A52–A55

Diagrams, reading and making, A6, A10, A28, A55, B8, B17, B21, B22, B23, C26, C30, C33, C55, C61, C73, D7, D19, D38, D47, E8, E15, E25, E27, E38, E40, E44, E45, E54, E56, F15, F42, F45*, F49, F57, F68, F72

Dictionary, using, A75

Digestive system, A62, A65, R28

Dinosaur, C24–25, C27

Distance, E7*, E9, E11, E56

Dragonfly, B9

Drawing conclusions, A5*, A11*, A12*, A15*, A20, A25*, A29, A39*, A51*, A61*, A66*, A69*, B5*, B11*, B25*, B41*, B49*, B56*, B59*, C5*, C13*, C16*, C21*, C29*, C37*, C53*, C69*, C71*, D5*, D15*, D20*, D23*, D35*, D45*, D50*, E5*, E13*, E18*, E23*, E37*, E43*, E53*, E58*, F5*, F9*, F13*, F19*, F20*, F25*, F33*, F41*, F53*, F58*, F63*, F65*, F71*

Droughts, B61

Dunes, C74

Dust Bowl, C66–67, C74

E

Ears, A64, A68, F68

Earth, C4–5*, C6–7*, C8–13*, C14–16*, C17–21*, C22–29*, C30–37*, C38–43*, C44–45, C52–53*, C54–59*, C60–65, C68–69*, C70–75, C78–79, D28–29, D36–40*, D41, D42–43, D46–49, D53*, D54–55, E16–17, F42, F60

compared to the Moon, D48–49

how it revolves, D38–39, D41

how it rotates, D36–41

resources of, C4–5*, C6–7*, C8–13*, C14–16*, C17–21*, C22–29*, C30–37*, C38–43*, C44–45

surface of, C30–31*, C32–35, C38, C52–53*, C54–59*, C60–64*, C68–69*, C70–75, C78–79, D28–29

Earthquakes, C72, C75

Ecologist, B70–71

Ecosystems, B4–5*, B6–10*, B11, B45, B58–59*, B60–67

changes in, B58–59*, B60–67

how they come back, B62–63

parts of, B6–7

small organisms of, B7

Egg, A48, A52–55, A57, A58–59, A72

Electrical flow, F72–75

Electric cars, C46–47

Electric circuit, F72–73*, F75

Electric current, F72, F75

Electricity, B47, C46–47, F70–71*, F72–75

Elements, F28–33

Embryo, A26–27*

Endangered species, B64–67

Endocrine systems, R34

Energy, A18, A40, B16, B46–47, E38–39, E40*–41, F16–17, F42–43, F48, F50–51, F60–61, F67–68, alternate sources of, B47

changes in, F48

food as source of, A40, B16

forms of, B47, E39

heat as, F42–43

how it is related to work, E38–39

of motion, E39

of sound, F67–68

saving, F50–51

stored, E39, E40

waves of, F60–61

Energy pyramid, B22–23

Environment, A8–9, A12*–13, A17*, A20–21, A46, B4–5*

Equator, D37

Erosion, C62, C64*, C65, C66–67

Esophagus, A62

Evaporation, C31, D17, D18, D20*, D21, F17, F19

Excretory system, R29

Expansion, F44–45*

Experiments, A12*, A13, A39*, A61*, B25*, B32*, B41*, B44*, B49*, B59*, C16*, C21*, C37*, C59*, C64*, C69*, D25*, D58*, E7*, E13*, E23*, E28*, E43*, E46*, E53*, F5*,

Explore activities - Inferring

F13*, F25*, F41*, F53*, F58*, F63*

Explore activities, A5*, A15*, A25*, A39*, A51*, A61*, A69*, B5*, B15*, B25*, B41*, B49*, B59*, C5*, C13*, C21*, C29*, C37*, C53*, C59*, C69*, D5*, D15*, D23*, D35*, D45*, D53*, E5*, E13*, E23*, E43*, E53*, F5*, F13*, F25*, F41*, F53*, F63*, F71*

Extinction, B66-67

Eyes, A64, A67

F

Fahrenheit scale, D8, R2, R11

Fertilizers, C43*

Fiberglass, F34-35

First quarter Moon, D46-47

Fish, A71, B8

Flashlight, F73*

Floods, B60, B61, C71

Flowering plants, A28, A31

Food chains, B14-15*, B16-19*, B20-23

Food pyramid, R27

Food webs, B20-21*, B22-23

Force, E12-13*, E14-18*, E26, E44, E46*-48, E55-56, F10, R3, R10

Forensic scientist, F79

Forest, B7, B10-11, B62, B67

Forest community, B10-11

Forest fires, B62, C42

Fossil, C20-21*, C22-27

Fossil fuels, C20-21*, C22-23*, C24-27, C38, C41, C45, C46-47, F50-51

Freezing, F17, F32

Friction, E26-27, E28*-29, E40

Frog, A52-53, A58-59, A72, B8, B46-47

Fuel, A40-41*, C26, C45

Fulcrum, E44-45, E46*-49, E50

Full Moon, D46-47

Fungi, B18

G

Gasohol, C45

Gases, A65, B12, B26-27, B34, C31, C38, C43*, C73, D6, D16-17, D51, F12-13*, F14-20*, F21, F28, F42, F65*

Gasoline, C46-47

Geology, C78-79

Germination, A26

Gills, A42, A71, B9

Glaciers, C55, C62, C65

Glass, C10, F34-35

Gneiss, C9

Gold, F27-28

Gram, F9*, R3

Grand Canyon, C57

Granite, C6

Graphite, C10

Graphs, making, R16-17. *See also* Bar graphs.

Grassland community, B6

Gravity, A32-33, D28-29, D48, E16-17, F10

Great Blue Heron, B9

Great Lakes, C56

Great Plains, C56-57, C66, C74, D12-13

Great Salt Lake, C30

Groundwater, C33, C35, D18-19

Growth and change, A6-7, A13, A26, A50-51*, A52-55

H

Habitats, B7-10*, B11, B60
    forest, B10*
    pond, B8-9

Health link, A67, D41

Heat, D8, D18, D55, F31, F40-41*, F42-45*, F46-49

Herbivore, B20

Heredity, A27*, A56*

Hibernation, A46

High pressure, D10, D26

Hills, C55

Honeycreeper, B50

Hooke, Robert, A10

Host, B31, B33

Humus, C14

Hurricanes, C70-71, C75

Hydrogen, F29, F30

Hypothesis, forming, C13*, C34, C64*, C69*, E23*, F13*, F65*

I

Igneous rock, C8-9

Immune system, R33

Imprints, C23*

Inclined plane, E51, E54, E56, E59

Inferring, A5*, A19*, A25*, A27*, A57*, A66*, B5*, B41*, B49*, B56*, B59*, C5*, C13*, C23*, C29*,

* Indicates an activity related to this topic.

C37*, C53*, C59*, C64*, C71*, D15*, D20*, D25*, D35*, D45*, E53*, E58*, F41*, F73*
Inherited traits, A56*
Inner planets, D56
Insects, A8, A28, A41, A46, A61*, B7, B8, B16, B22, B51
Insulators, F46–47, F49
Internet, using. See Technology link.
Interview, conducting, B33, D41
Intestines, A62
Invertebrates, A70, A75
Iron, F27, F28, F30, F31

J

Jet stream, D7
Jupiter, D54, D56–57, D59

K

Kilogram, F9*

L

Lake, C29*, C30, C33, C42, C52, C55–56, D18
Landforms, C52–53*, C54–55, C57, C69*
Landslides, C72
Language Arts link, A75
Last quarter Moon, D46–47
Lava, C73
Leaves, A16, A18, A21, A22, B7

Learned traits, A56*
Length, F59, R2, R7
Lenses, D58*, F56, R4
Levers, E44–45, E46*, E49, E50
Life cycles, A24–25*, A26–27*, A28–31, A52–55. See also Animals, Plants.
Light, F52–53*, F54–59, F60
  defining, F54
  how it bends, F56, F58*
  how it reflects, F55, F57, F59
  how it travels, F54–55, F60–61
  opaque materials, F54
  rays of, F54–56, F59
  refractions, F56
  shadows, F54, F59
  using, F59
Limestone, C7
Line graph, R17
Liquids, C31, D16–18, F12–13*, F14–20*, F21, F28, F65*, R9
List, making, A67, A69*, B10*, B11, B15*, B23, B33, B56, E59, F53*, F69
Liter, F9*, R3
Literature link, A21, A57, B33, B45, B67, C45, D27, D51, D59, E11, E19, E49, F21, F33, F75
Living things
  adaptations of, B48–49*, B50–56*, B57
  cells of, A10–11*, A62–63
  changes in, A6–9, A12*, A13
  characteristics of, A27*
  communication of, A9
  comparing, A4–5*, A13

  competition of, B40–41*, B42–45
  endangering, B64–67
  environment of, A8–9, A12*, A20–21
  extinction of, B66–67
  features of, A4–5*, A6–7, A13
  growth of, A6–7, A13, A26, A50–51*, A52–55
  habitats of, B7–10, B45
  life cycles of, A24–25*, A26–27*, A28–31, A52–55
  needs of, A14–15*, A16–19*, A21, A24–25*, A38–39*, A40–47, A65, B24–25*, B26–27
  parts of, A40–41*, A60–61, A62–66, B9
  recycling, B18–19*, B23, B33
  relationships among, B4–B5*, B6–10*, B11, B12–13, B14–15*, B16–19*, B20–25*, B26–32*, B33, B34–35
  reproduction of, A7, A13, A26–27*, A28–31, B32*, B33, B51
  responses of, A8–9, A12*, A13, A20–21, A45–47
  smaller parts of, A10–11*
Load, E44–45, E46*, E48–49, E54
Loam, C15, C17
Loggerhead turtle, B64
Low pressure, D10, D26
Lunar calendar, D48
Luster, F6

Machines, E42–43*, E44–46*,
E47–51, E53*, E54–58*, E59
  compound, E57, E59
  simple, E44–51, E53*,
    E54–58*, E59
Magnetism, F26
Magnets, F25*–26, F33
Mammals, A74–75
Maps, reading and making,
  B11, B23, C65, D11, D26,
  E10, E11, R18
  map key and symbols, E10
Marble, C9
Marine geologist, C78–79
Mars, D54, D56–57, D59
Mass, F7–8, F9*–11, R2–3
Math link, A13, A21, A75,
  B11, B33, B45, B57, B67,
  C11, C17, C27, C35, C57,
  C65, C75, D11, D21, D41,
  D51, E11, E29, E49, F11,
  F33, F59, F69
Matter, D16, F4–5*, F6–11,
  F12–13*, F14–20*, F21,
  F24–25*, F27–28, F30,
  F60–61
  building blocks of, F24–25*
  changes in, F16–17
  classifying, F14–15
  definite volume, F14–15
  describing, F6
  forms of, F12–13*,
    F14–20*, F21
  mixtures, F18
  properties of, F6, F7–F11,
    F25*, F27, F28, F30
  smallest particle of, F28
  solutions, F19
Mealworm, A12*
Measuring, A5*, A19*, B5*,
  C16*, D22, D23*, D24,

D40*, E4*, E5*, E7*, E8–9,
  E11, E13*, E53*, E58*,
  F8–9*, F59*, R2–3, R6–11
  distance, E7*, E11
  force, R10
  length, F59*, R7
  mass and volume, F8–9*,
    R3, R8–9
  motion, E8
  speed, E5*, E9
  temperature, D23*, D24,
    R11
  time, R6
  units of measurement, R2
  weight, R10
  wind speed and direction,
    D24
Meet People in Science,
  A78–79, B70–71, C78–79,
  D62–63, E62–63, F78–79
Melting, F17, F32
Mercury, D54, D56–57, D59
Mesas, C55, C57
Mesosphere, D7
Metals, C41, F26–27
Metamorphic rock, C9
Metamorphosis, A52–53, A57
Meters, R2–3
Metric system, E17, R2–3
Microscope, A10, R5
Migration, A46, A48–49
Mimicry, B53
Minerals, A16, C6–7*,
  C8–11, C14–15, C38*, C41
Mineral scratch test, C7*
Mining, B34, C36–37*, C38
Mirror, F55, R5
Mixtures, F18–19, F21,
  F34–35
Models, making, B25*, B49*,
  C23*, C29*, C36*, C43*,
  C69, D15*, D20, D35*,
  D45*, D53*, F49

Molds, C23
Monarch butterfly, A48–49,
  A52–53
Moon, D28–29, D44–45*,
  D46–51, E17, F10
  compared to Earth,
    D48–49
  phases of, D46–47
Mosses, A17, A22–23
Motion, D11, E8, E14, E23*,
  E24, E38–39
Mountains, A44, B11, C52,
  C55–56
Mount Saint Helens, B60, B63
Mouth, A62, A65, A67
Movement, D10, D34–35*,
  D36–40*, D41, E5*–7*,
  E20–21, E26–27, E47
  how things move, E5*–7*
  of air, D10
  of Earth, D34–35*,
    D36–40*, D41
  what makes it stop,
    E26–27
Moving parts, A64, E20–21
Muscular system, A62,
  E20–21, R23
Music link, C45

NASA, A32–33, E62–63
National Geographic
  Amazing Stories, A32–33,
  B34–35, C46–47, D28–29,
  E30–31, F34–35
Natural disasters, B64
Natural gas, C41
Naturalist, B71
Natural resources, C38–43*,
  D21

* Indicates an activity related to this topic.

Nectar, A28

Needs, of living things, A14–15*, A16–19*, A38–39*, A41–41*, A42–43

Neptune, D54, D56–57, D59

Nerve cells, A62

Nervous system, A62, R30

New Moon, D46–47

Newton, E17, F10

Niche, B44–B45

Night, D34–35*, D36–37, D41

Nitrogen, C18

Nonliving things, B5*, B6–7, C4–5*, C6–11, C14–15, C33, C41, C60, C62, C78–79, F28–33

Nonrenewable resources, C41, C45

Northern lights, D7

North pole, C30, D8, D37, D38

Nose, A65

Nuclear energy, B47

Nucleus, A10–A11*

Numbers, using, A11*, C34*, E58*

Nutrients, A22–23

O

Observations, making, A5*, A15*, A19*, A25*, A27*, A39*, A51*, A61*, A75*, B5*, B10*, B15*, B19*, B25*, B56*, C5*, C7*, C13*, C21*, C29*, C37*, C53*, C59*, C64*, C69*, D9*, D15*, D25*, D35*, D53*, D58*, E13*, E28*, E39*, F5*, F13*, F20*, F25*, F45*, F63*

Ocean, A44, B16, C30, C55, C78–79, D18, D28–29

Oil, B46, C26, C38, C41

Omnivore, B21

Opaque materials, F54

Open circuit, F73*

Orbit, D38, D46–47, D56

Organ, A62, A67

Organisms, A4–12*, A13–21, A38–47, A52–57, A60–69, A70–75, B4–33, B40–45, B48–67

decomposers, B18–19*

features of, A5*–7

hosts and parasites, B31

how they are affected by change, B60–67

how they are put together, A62–66*

how they perish, B63

largest, B27

one–celled, B18–19*

relocation of, B63

responses of, A8–9, A12*, A13, A20–21, A45–47

See also Animals, Living things, Plants.

Orion, D42–43

Outer planet, D56–D57

Oxygen, A19*, A42–43, A65, A71, B12, B26–27, B33, B34, C38, F29–31

Oxygen cycle, B27, B33

P

Paleontology, C79

Parasite, B31

Patterns, C5*, D50*, F15

Periodic table, F27

Perish, B63

Phases, D46–47

Physical change, F16, F21, F32–33

Pictograph, R17

Pitch, F66

Plains, C55–57

Planetary rings, D57

Planets, D52–53*, D54–57, D59

Plants, A4–5*, A6–8, A11, A13, A14–23, A24–25*, A26, A27*–31, A32–33, B12–13, B16–17, B22, B24–27, B32, B34–35, B40–46, B51, C25–26, C38, C40

as producers, B16–17, B22

conifers, A29

flowering, A28, A31

how humans depend on, B12–13

how they are helped by animals, A28, B26–27, B32

how they compete with animals, B40–41*, B42–46

life cycle of, A24–25*, A26

needs of, A14–15*, A16–19*, A21, A25*, A26, B24–25*, B26–27

parts of A16–18, A21

reproduction of, A27*–31, B32, B51

responses to environment, A20–21

simple, A17

Plastics, F22–23

Plateau, C55, C57

Plow, E55

Pluto, D54, D56–57, D59

Pollen, A28

Pollination, A28

Pollution, B64, B66, C42, C43*

Pond ecosystems, B8–9

Population, B6–9, B11, B28–31

Position, E6, E8, E10, E11

Position words, E6

Pounds, E17, R3

Precipitation, D18–19, D24

Predator, B28–29, B33, B42, B52–54, B59

Predicting, A5*, A11*, A12*, A15*, A20*, A25*, A29*, A39*, A51*, A61*, A66*, A69*, B32*, B41*, B49*, B59*, C7*, C21*, C29*, C53*, C59*, D9*, D20*, D23*, D50*, D53*, E4*, E13*, E23*, F5*, F9*, F25*, F41*, F53*, F71*

Prey, B28–29, B33, B42, B52

Prism, F57

Problem solving, A13, A75, B11, B45, B57, C17, D21, D41, E11

Process Skill Builder, A12*, A66*, B10*, B56*, C16*, C64*, D20*, D50*, E18*, E58*, F20*, F50*

Producers, B16–17, B19

Properties
of living things, A4–5*, A6–7, A13
of matter F4–5*, F6–9*, F10–18
of rocks, C6–7*

Pulley, E48

Pulls, D14–16, E12–13*, E19, E20–21, F10

Pupa, A52–53

Pushes, E12, E14–16, E20–21, E38–39, F10

Q

Quick Lab, A11*, A19*, A27*, A41*, A56*, A73*, B9*, B32*, B44*, B65*, C7*, C23*, C43*, C55*, C61*, C71*, D40*, E7*, E46*, F9*, F45*, F73*, F67*

R

Rain, A22, C29*, C31–32, C66, C68–69*, C70–72, C75

Rain gauge, D24

Rain forest, A78–79, B34–35, B43, B66

Ramp, E51, E53*–54

Reading skills
cause and effect, C56, C63, C71, D40*, D49, D57
comparing and contrasting, A46, A54, A63, A72, B43, B55, B57, B66, E39, E48, E57
main idea, A6, A16, A26, A40, A52, A62, A70, B6, B16, B26, B42, B50, B60, C6, C22, C30, C38, C54, C60, C70, D6, D16, D24, D36, D46, D54, E6, E7*, E9, E14, E16, E24, E28*, E38, E44, E54, F6, F14, F26, F42, F54, F64, F72
sequence of events, C10, C15, C23*, C31, C43*, F45, F55, F65, F73
summarizing, B7, B19*, B32, D10, D17, D24

Recycling, B18–19*, C44–45, F34–35

Reducing, C44–45

Reflection, F55, F57, F59

Refracts, F56

Relationships, among living things, B4–5*, B6–10*, B11, B12–13, B14–15*, B16–19*, B20–25*, B26–32*, B33, B34–35

Relocation, B63

Renewable resources, B47, C40, C45, F34–35

Reproduction, A7, A26–27*, A28–31, A52–55, A74, B51

Reptiles, A72

Research, A31, C26, D59, E41, E49, F11, F33, F49, F75

Reservoirs, C32

Resources, B47, C34*, C35, C36–37*, C38–43*, C44–45;
See conservation

Respiratory system, R26

Responses, of living things, A8, A12*, A20

Reusing, C44–45

Revolution, D38–39, D41, D42–43, D48, D54

Rivers, B11, B61, C55–56

Rocks, C4–5*, C6–11, C14–15, C33, C41, C60, C62, C78–79
comparing, C5*
how they are formed, C8–9
how we use them, C10–11
properties of, C6–7*

Roots, A16–17, A26

Rotation, D36–37, D41, D48, D54–57

Rust, F30–31

* Indicates an activity related to this topic.

S

Salt, F19, F30
Salt water, C30
Sand dune, C55
Sapling, A6
Satellite, D46
Saturn, D54, D56–57, D59
Scavengers, B29
Science Magazine, A22–23, A48–49, A58–59, B12–13, B46–47 ,C18–19, C66–67, D12–13, D42–43, E20–21, E50–51, F22–23, F50–51, F60–61
Screw, E56, E58*
Seasons, D38–39, D40*, D41
Sedimentary rock, C8–9, C22
Seedling, A27
Seeds, A5*, A24–25*, A26–31, B60
Seismic waves, F60
Senses, A9, A13, A64, B28, R31–32
Shade, A22, A27*
Shadow, F54, F59
Shelter, A44, B7–8
Silt, C14, C15
Siltstone, C10
Silver, F27–28
Simple machines, E42–43*, E44–46*, E47–49, E50–51, E53*, E54–58*, E59
Skeletal system, R20–22
Skin, A63–65, A67
Snake, A72
Social studies link, A31, A75, B11, B23, C27, C57, C65, C75, D27, D59, E41, E49, E59, F11, F21, F49, F75
Sodium, F30

Sodium chloride, F19, F30
Soil, A8, A32, C10, C12–13*, C14–15*, C16–18, C30, C33, C60, C66–67
as natural resource, C38
as renewable resource, C40
defining, C13*
kinds of, C15
layers of, C14
Solar cells, B47
Solar energy, B47
Solar system, D54–55
Solids, D16–17, F12–13*, F14–20*, F21, F28, F65
Solution, F19, F21
Sound, F60–61, F62–63*, F64–69
changes in, F66, F69
how it is heard, F68
how it travels, F60–61, F65*, F68
making, F63*, F64
pitch of, F66
vibration of, F64–66, F68
volume of, F67
South Pole, C30, D8, D37, D38
Space, A32–33, B41*, B42–44*, B45–47, F6–9, F42, R9
Speed, E9–10, R3
Sphere, D36, D46, D48
Spores, A30
Star, D42–43, D55
Steel, C27, F19, F27
Stem, A16–17, A26
Stomach, A62
Stored energy, E39, E40
Stratosphere, D7
Subsoil, C14, C17
Summarizing, B19*

Sun, A18, A22–23, B47, D8, D18, D34, D36–40*, D41, D42–43, D46, D52–53*, D54–55, F42–44, F54, F60
Survey, conducting, E59
Survival, B63*–65
Switch, electrical, F73*, F75
Systems
body, A62–63, R20–34
electrical, F72–75

T

Tables, making and reading, C57, F20*, F21, F58*, R18–19
Tadpole, A52–53, A58
Tarter, Dr. Jill, D62–63
Technology link, A13, A21, A23, A31, A33, A47, A57, A67, A75, B11, B13, B23, B33, B35, B45, B47, B57, B67, C11, C17, C19, C27, C35, C45, C57, C65, C75, C79, D11, D21, D29, D41, D51, D59, D63, E11, E19, E29, E41, E49, E59, E63, F11, F21, F33, F49, F51, F59, F61, F69, F75, F79
Telescope, D58*, D59
Temperate forest, B43
Temperature, A26, A48, A71, A74, C60, D8, D11, D20*, D23*, D26, D27, F13*, F43, F44, F48, F49, R2–3, R11
Terrace farming, C66
Texture, F6
Thermometer, D8, D23*, D24, D27, F43–45*, F49, R11
Think and write, A13, A21, A31, A47, A57, A67, A75,

B11, B23, B33, B45, B57, B67, C11, C17, C27, C35, C45, C57, C65, C75, D11, D21, D41, D51, D59, E11, E19, E29, E41, E49, E59, F11, F21, F33, F49, F59, F69, F75

Threads, of a screw, E56, E58

Tides, D28–29

Tilted axis, D37–39, D41

Time, D36, D40*, D48, R6

Tissue, A62, A67

Topsoil, C14, C17

Tornado, C70–71*, C75, D12

Traits, A56*

Trash, C43*, C45–46

Tree, A6, A17, A24, A28, B7, B27, C66

Troposphere, D6–7

Tubers, A30

Tundra, B55

Turtle, A55

Unbalanced forces, E24–25

Unequal forces, E24–25

Uranus, D54, D56–57, D59

Valley, C55

Variables,using, F58*, F59

Venus, D54, D56–57, D59

Venus flytrap, A22–23

Vertebrates, A70, A75

Vibration, F64–66, F68

Vocabulary words, A4, A14, A24, A38, A50, A60, A68, B4, B14, B24, B40, B48, B58, C4, C12, C20, C28, C36, C52, C58, C68, D4, D14, D22, D34, D44, D52, E4, E12, E22, E36, E42, E52, F4, F12, F24, F40, F52, F62, F70

Volcanoes, B60–61, C8, C42, C73, C75, C78–79

Volume, F7–8, F14, F67, R3, R9

of objects, F7–8, F14, R3, R9

of sound, F67

Warm-blooded animals, A74

Waste gas, A65

Wastes, A65, C43*, C45–46, R29

Water, A8, A19, A22–23, A26, A40, A42–43, A45, A65, B7–8, B11, B47, C16*, C28–34*, C35, C38, C40, C43*, C60, C63, D14–15*, D16–20*, D49, F29

Water cycle, C31, C35, C40, D14–15*, D18–21

Water pollution, A58

Water vapor, C31, D17–18, F17

Weather, D6–7, D12–13, D22–23*, D24–29

describing, D22–23*, D24–29

Weather map, D26

Weather satellites, D27

Weather vane, D24–25*

Weathering, C60–61*, C64*–65, C74

Wedge, E55

Weight, E17, F10, R2–3, R10

Wetland, C63

Wheel and axle, E47, E57

Wildlife conservationist, A78–79

Wind, A28, B47, B60, C66, C70–71, C74–75, D10–11, D12–13, D24–25*

Wind energy, B47

Windlass, E47

Woolly mammoth, C25, C27

Work, A40, E36–37*, E38–39, E43*–49, E50–51, E54–58*, E59

ability to, A40

how it is related to energy, E38–39

making it easier, E43*–49, E50–51, E54–59

Wright, Dr. Dawn, C78–79

Writing link, A13, A21, A31, A47, A57, A67, B11, B23, B33, B45, B57, B67, C17, C27, C35, C57, C65, C75, D21, D41, D51, D59, E11, E19, E29, E41, E59, F33, F49, F69

* Indicates an activity related to this topic.

Credits

Cover Design and Illustration: Robert Brook Allen

Cover Photos: Kim Taylor/Bruce Coleman/Natural Selection, (bg) Darrell Gulin/Stone, (l) © PhotoSpin 2000

Illustrations: Dolores Bego: p. E10; Frank Comito: p. R6; Barbara Cousins: pp. E21, R25, R27, (l) R28, R29; Daniel DelValle: p. B5; Jeff Fagen: pp. E27, E33; Function Through Form: p. F29; Peter Gunther: pp. C14,C26, C30, C31, C33, C61, C73, D7, D8, D10, D18, D31, D40, D42, E17, F8, F15, F42, F57, F63, F72; Colin Hayes: pp. A41, E44, E48, E48, E54, E55, E60, E61, R5, R7, R9, R16, R17, R18, (l) R19; John Karapelou: pp. R30, R32, (m) R33, (b) R33; Yuan Lee: B7, B8, B16, F68, F77; Tom Leonard: pp. R20,R21, R22, R23; Kevin O'Malley: pp. E25, F10, F11; Joe LeMonnier: pp. B64, C56, D11, D13, D26, D36, D37, D47, D61; Steve Oh: pp. A62, R26, R27, (r) R28, R29, R31, R34; Sharon O'Neil: p. C47; Precision Graphics: pp. A28, A29, A42, A71; Pat Rasch: pp. E56, E57, E58; Molly Scanlon: pp. F7, F64, F66, F74; Rob Schuster: p. F73; Neecy Twinem: pp. B10, B20; Olivia: pp. R2, R3, R9, R10, R11, R14, R15, (r) R19, Patricia Wynne: pp. S4, S5, R24, (r) R33; J/B Woolsey Associates: pp. A10, A11, C54, C76; Josie Yee: pp. D38, D54;

Photography Credits: All photographs are by the Macmillan/McGraw-Hill School Division (MMSD) and Michael Groen, Dan Howell, Ken Karp, Dave Mager, John Serafin for MMSD except as noted below.

Contents: iv: Photodisc. v: (l) Runk/Schoenberger/Grant Heilman Photography, Inc.; (r) Photodisc. vi: (l) Francois Gohier/Photo Researchers, Inc.; (r) American Museum of Natural History. vii: (l) NASA/Photo Researchers, Inc.; (r) John Sanford/Photo Researchers, Inc. viii: Peter Weimann/Animals Animals. ix: D. Boone/Corbis.

National Geographic Invitation to Science: S1: (bg) Greig Cranna/Stock • Boston; (i) Mark A. Madison. S2: Mark A. Madison. S3: (t) NASA/Peter Arnold Inc.; (b) Mark A. Madison. S7: Ken Karp. S8: (br) PhotoDisc.

National Geographic Unit Opener A: A0: Clive Druett/Papilio/Corbis. A1: Victoria McCormick/Animals Animals. **Unit A:** A2: Alan Oddie/PhotoEdit. A4: Douglas Peebles/Corbis. A5: Ken Karp. A6: (t) Terry Eggers/The Stock Market; (l) Tony Wharton/Corbis; (r) The Stock Market; (b) Terry Eggers/The Stock Market. A7: (l) Frank Siteman/Stock • Boston; (tr) Photodisc; (mr) Photodisc; (br) Photodisc. A8: (t) Gerard Fuehrer/DRK Photo; SuperStock. A9: (tl) Norbert Wu/Peter Arnold Inc.; (tr) Secret Sea Visions/Peter Arnold Inc.; (b) Joe McDonald/Visuals Unlimited. A10: (t) Ken Wood/Photo Researchers, Inc.; (b) Dwight R. Kuhn. A11: (t) Ken Karp; (b) Moredun Animal Health LTD/Science Photo Library/Photo Researchers, Inc. A12: Ken Karp. A13: Cart Roessler/Animals Animals. A14: (bg) PhotoDisc; (tl) Doug Peebles/Panoramic Images; (tr) Allen Prier/Panoramic Images; (m) Mark Segal/Panoramic Images. A15: Ken Karp. A16: (bg) Runk/Schoenberger/Grant Heilman Photography; (i) E. Webber/Visuals Unlimited. A17: (l) Jim Zipp/Photo Researchers, Inc.; (r) Jenny Hager/The Image Works. A18: (l) Runk/Schoenberger/Grant Heilman Photography; (r) C.G. Van Dyke/Visuals Unlimited. A19: (t) Dave M. Phillips/Visuals Unlimited; (b) Ken Karp. A20: (t) Bill Beatty/Visuals Unlimited; (b) Pat O'Hara/DRK Photo. A22: (bg) Randy Green/FPG International; (l) Stan Osolinski/Dembinsky Photo Assoc.; (r) Larry West/FPG International. A23: (t) John M. Roberts/The Stock Market; (b) J. H. Robinson/Photo Researchers, Inc. A24: Neil Gilchrist/Panoramic Images. A25: Ken Karp. A26: (t) D. Gavagnaro/Visuals Unlimited; (tm) Kevin Collins/Visuals Unlimited; (bm) Tony Freeman/PhotoEdit; (bl) Inga Spence/Tom Stack & Associates; (br) Inga Spence/Visuals Unlimited. A27: D. Gavagnaro/Visuals Unlimited. A29: Gerald and Buff Corsi/Visuals Unlimited. A30: (t) David Young-Wolfe/PhotoEdit; (m) David Young-Wolfe/PhotoEdit; (bl) Ed Reschke/Peter Arnold Inc.; (br) Jeff J. Daly/Visuals Unlimited. A31: Inga Spence/Visuals Unlimited. A32: Ed Galindo. A33: (t) Ed Galindo; (b) C Squared Studios/PhotoDisc. A36: Stephen J. Krasemann/Photo Researchers, Inc. A38: Jade Albert/FPG International. A39: Ken Karp. A40: (t) Fritz Polikng/Bruce Coleman Inc.; (bl) Joe McDonald/DRK Photo; (br) Dale E. Boyer/Photo Researchers, Inc. A41: Kevin Schafer/Peter Arnold Inc. A42: (i) W. Gregory Brown/Animals Animals; (t) Ken Karp; (b) Michael S. Nolan/Tom Stack & Associates. A43: Ken Karp. A44: (t) Eric & David Hosking/Corbis; (m) John Cancalosi/DRK Photo; (b) Ted Levine/Animals Animals. A45: (t) Zoran Milich/Allsport USA; (b) Mark Newman/Bruce Coleman Inc. A46: (t) David Madison/Bruce Coleman Inc.; (m) Runk/Schoenberger/Grant Heilman Photography; (b) John Cancalosi/DRK Photo. A48: (bg) Ken Lucas/Visuals Unlimited; (t) Skip Moody/Dembinsky Photo Assoc.; (b) Skip Moody/Dembinsky Photo Assoc. A49: (tl) Skip Moody/Dembinsky Photo Assoc.; (tr) Skip Moody/Dembinsky Photo Assoc.; (m) Jon Dicus; (b) Skip Moody/Dembinsky Photo Assoc. A50: Tim Davis/Photo Researchers, Inc. A51: Ken Karp. A52: (t) Dwight R. Kuhn; (b) Arthur Morris/Visuals Unlimited. A53: (tl) Gelnn M. Oliver/Visuals Unlimited; (tr) Robert P. Carr/Bruce Coleman Inc.; (tm) Pat Lynch/Zipp/Photo Researchers, Inc.; (ml) Nuridsany et Perennou/Zipp/Photo Researchers, Inc.; (mr) Robert L. Dunne/Bruce Coleman Inc.; (bl) Sharon Cummings/Dembinsky Photo Assoc.; (br) John Mielcarek/Dembinsky Photo Assoc. A54: (t) SuperStock; (mr) Lynn Rogers/Peter Arnold Inc.; (bl) Erwin and Peggy Bauer/Bruce Coleman Inc.; (br) Pat and Tom Leeson/Photo Researchers, Inc. A55: (t) Cabisco/Visuals Unlimited; (ml) E.A. Janes/Bruce Coleman Inc; (mr) Lindholm/Visuals Unlimited; (bm) Fred Breummer/DRK Photo; (bl) M H Sharp/Photo Researchers, Inc; (br) Dave B. Fleetham/Visuals Unlimited. A56: (t) Ken Karp; (bl) George Shelley/The Stock Market; (br) Richard Hutchings/PhotoEdit. A58: (bg) J.C. Carton/Bruce Coleman Inc.; (i) Bill Banaszewski/Visuals Unlimited. A60: Robert Maier/Animals Animals. A61: Ken Karp. A62: (t) Ken Karp; (b) M.I. Walker/Science Source/Photo Researchers, Inc. A63: (t) R. Dowling/Animals Animals; (b) Joe McDonald/Animals Animals. A64: (t) Robert Winslow; (b) Tom Brakefield/Corbis. A65: (t) James Watt/Animals Animals; (b) Jeff Rotman/Jeff Rotman Photography. A66: Photodisc. A68: VCG/FPG International. A69: (t) Stephen Dalton/Animals Animals; (tm) Tony Wharton/Corbis; (m) G.W.Willis/Animals Animals; (ml) Eye Wire; (mr) Brian Parker/Tom Stack & Associates; (bl) Kichen and Hurst/Tom Stack & Associates; (br) Lisa and Mike Husar/DRK Photo. A70: (l) Darryl Torckler/Tony Stone Images; (r) Rob Simpson/Visuals Unlimited. A71: (i) George Bernard/Animals Animals; (t) Breck P. Kent/Animals Animals. A72: (t) Jane Borton/Bruce Coleman Inc.; (b) E.R. Degginger/Animals Animals. A73: (l) S. Nielson/DRK Photo; (r) Robert Winslow. A74: (t) Jeff Rotman/Jeff Rotman Photography; (b) Dave Watts/Tom Stack & Associates. A75: (t) Erwin & Peggy Bauer/Bruce Coleman Inc.; (b) Lynn M. Stone/Bruce Coleman Inc. A77: (l) SuperStock; (r) SuperStock. A78: (bg) Michael Fogden/DRK Photo; (i) Dr. Fransisco Gomez-Dallmeier. A80: (tl) David Young-Wolfe/PhotoEdit; (tr) Jeff J. Daly/Visuals Unlimited.

National Geographic Unit Opener B: B00: Tim Flach/Tony Stone. B0 Christer Fredriksson/Natural Selection Stock Photography. B1 Tim Davis/Tony Stone. **Unit B:** B2: (bg) Corbis; (l) John Gerlach/Visuals Unlimited; (m) David M. Schleser/Photo Researchers, Inc.; (r) Tony Stone Images. B4: Johnny Johnson/Animals Animals. B5: Photodisc. B6: (t) Nicholas DeVore/Tony Stone Images; (b) Joseph Van Os/Image Bank. B12: (i) Lance Nelson/The Stock Market; (m) Jeff Greenberg/Visuals Unlimited; (b) Jeff Greenberg/PhotoEdit. B13: (i) PhotoDisc; (t) Gerard Lacz/Peter Arnold Inc.; (b) PhotoDisc. B14: (bg) L. Lenz/Natural Selection. B16: Kim Taylor/Dorling Kindersley Ltd. B18: (i) Runk/Schoenberger /Grant Heilman Photography; (t) SuperStock; (bl) Tom Bean/DRK Photo; (br) Kim Taylor/Dorling Kindersley Ltd. B19: (l) Michael P. Gadomski/Photo Researchers, Inc. B22: (t) John Warden/Tony Stone Images; (tm) Tom J. Ulrich/Visuals Unlimited; (bm) John Shaw/Bruce Coleman Inc; (b) Runk/Schoenberger/Grant Heilman Photography, Inc. B23: Jim Steinberg/Photo Researchers, Inc. B24: (bg) Michael Simpson/FPG International. B26: (bg) Kent Foster/Photo Researchers, Inc; (i) William H. Mullins/Photo Researchers, Inc. B28: (ti) John Shaw/Bruce Coleman Inc.; (t) Kim Taylor/Dorling Kindersley Ltd.; (tm) Kim Taylor/Dorling Kindersley Ltd.; (ml) Arthur Morris/The Stock Market.; (mr) M. C. Chamberlain/DRK Photo; (b) Kim Taylor/Dorling Kindersley Ltd. B29: (t) Jeremy Woodhouse/PhotoDisc; (b) Jerry Young/Dorling Kindersley Ltd. B30: (tl) Nawrocki Stock Photo; (b) Carl Roessler/Bruce Coleman Inc. B31: (tr) S. Dimmitt/Photo Researchers, Inc; (m) James H. Robinson/Photo Researchers, Inc.; (bl) Tony Stone Images; (br) Runk/Schoenberger/Grant Heilman Photography, Inc. B32: (r) Kim Taylor/Dorling Kindersley Ltd. B34: (bg) John Elk III; (ti) Trevor Barrett/Earth Scenes; (bi) George D. Lepp/Photo Researchers, Inc. B35: Kjell B. Sandved/Visuals Unlimited. B37: (l) Runk/Schoenberger/Grant Heilman Photography, Inc.; (m) Runk/Schoenberger/Grant Heilman Photography, Inc; (r) Arthur Morris/Visuals Unlimited. B38: Robert Winslow. B40: (bg) The Stock Market. B42: (t) Stephen Dalton/Animals Animals; (b) Richard Day/Panoramic Images. B43: (tl) Steve Maslowski/Visuals Unlimited; (tr) James P. Rowan/DRK Photo; (tr) George D. Dodge/Bruce Coleman Inc.; (br) Michael Dwyer/Stock • Boston. B44: (t) Gail Shumway/FPG International; (b) Ken Karp. B45: (l) Ken Lax/Photo Researchers, Inc. B46: (t) M.L. Sinibaldi/The Stock Market; (b) H.P. Merten/The Stock Market. B47: Larry Ulrich/DRK Photo. B48: (bg) Johnny Johnson/DRK Photo; (t) Tom and Pat Leeson/DRK Photo; (b) Richard &Susan Day/Animals Animals. B50: (t) Gail Shumway/FPG International; (m) Jack Jeffrey/Photo Resource Hawaii.; (b) John Cancalosi/DRK Photo. B51: (tl) Francis/Donna

Caldwell/Visuals Unlimited; (tr) Jack Hollingsworth/Photodisc; (b) Kim Taylor/Bruce Coleman Inc. B52: (t) Gregory Ochoki/Photo Researchers, Inc.; (b) Breck P. Kent/Animals Animals. B53: (t) Stephen J. Krasemann/DRK Photo; (m) A. Cosmos Blank/Photo Researchers, Inc.; (b) John Eastcott/Yva Momatiuk/DRK Photo. B54: (t) Zig Leszcynski/Animals Animals; (m) MIchael Fogden/DRK Photo; (b) MIchael Fogden/DRK Photo. B55: (tl) Pat O'Hara/DRK Photo; (tr) Richard Kolar/Animals Animals; (tm) Don Enger/Animals Animals; (bl) Jim Steinberg/Photo Researchers, Inc.; (br) Stephen J. Krasemann/Photo Researchers, Inc. B56: Ken Karp. B57: Chris Johns/National Geographic. B58: (bg) Gary Braasch/Corbis. B59: Ken Karp. B60: (t) Charles Palek/Earth Scenesphic; (b) Pat and Tom Lesson/Photo Researchers, Inc. B61: (l) Robert Madden/National Geographicphic; (r) Jim Hughes/Visuals Unlimited. B62: (t) Diana L. Stratton/Tom Stack & Associates; (tm) Doug Sokell/Visuals Unlimited; (l) Kent and Donna Dannen/Photo Researchers, Inc.; (bm) Sharon Gerig/Tom Stack & Associates; (b) Pat and Tom Lesson/DRK Photo. B63: (t) Joe & Carol McDonald/Visuals Unlimited; (b) Stephen J. Krasemann/DRK Photo. B64: (t) M.C. Chamberlain/DRK Photo; (bl) Erwin and Peggy Bauer/Bruce Coleman Inc.; (br) G. Prance/Visuals Unlimited. B65: (b) M.C. Chamberlain/DRK Photo. B66: (t) Stephen J. Krasemann/DRK Photo; (b) Science VU/Visuals Unlimited. B67: (t) Barbara Gerlach/Visuals Unlimited. B69: (l) Pat and Tom Lesson/Photo Researchers, Inc.; (r) Robert Madden/National Geographic. B70: (t) Christina Allen. B71: Myleen Ferguson/PhotoEdit.

National Geographic Unit Opener C: C0: Donovan Reese/Tony Stone. C1: David Muench/Tony Stone. **Unit C:** C2: David Muench/Corbis. C4: (bg) Chip Porter/Tony Stone Images. C5: Ken Karp. C6: (t) Joyce Photographics/Photo Researchers, Inc.; (m) Runk/Schoenberger/Grant Heilman Photography; (b) Bill Bachmann/Index Stock Imagery. C7: (t) Tom Pantages; (m) Tom Pantages; (b) Ken Karp. C8: Adam G. Sylvester/Photo Researchers, Inc. C9: (tl) Ken Karp; (tr) S. Callahan/Visuals Unlimited; (tml) Joyce Photographics/Photo Researchers, Inc.; (tmr) Runk/Schoenberger/Grant Heilman Photography; (bl) Charles R. Belinky/Photo Researchers, Inc.; (br) Ken Karp. C10: (t) Frederik D. Bodin/Stock • Boston; (m) Erich Lessing/Art Resource; (b) Boleslaw Edelhajt/Gamma-Liaison. C12: (bg) Bo Brannhage/Panoramic Images. C13: Ken Karp. C14: Larry Lefever/Grant Heilman Photography. C15: (t) Stephen Ogilvy; (m) Ken Karpgilvy; (r) Ken Karp. C16: Ken Karp. C17: (l) George Lepp/Corbis; (r) Runk/Schoenberger/Grant Heilman Photography. C18: (tl) Roy Morsch/The Stock Market; (tr) Roy Morsch/The Stock Market; (m) The National Archives/Corbis; (bm) Roy Morsch/The Stock Market; (b) G. Buttner/Okapia/Photo Researchers, Inc. C19: Arthur C. Smith/Grant Heilman Photography. C20: (bg) Jeff J. Daly/Visuals Unlimited. C21: Ken Karp. C22: Tom Bean/DRK Photo. C23: (t) Runk/Schoenberger/Grant Heilman Photography; (b) Ken Karp. C24: (i) Mehau Kulyk/Photo Researchers, Inc.; (t) Louis Psihoyos/Matrix; (b) Fracois Gohier/Photo Researchers, Inc. C25: (l) Stephen J. Krasemann/DRK Photo; (m) Biophoto Associates/Photo Researchers, Inc.; (r) Stephen J. Krasemann/DRK Photo. C26: Ray Ellis/Photo Researchers, Inc. C28: (bg) F. Stuart Westmorland/Photo Researchers, Inc. C29: Ken Karp. C30: Tom Van Sant/Photo Researchers, Inc. C32: (t) Davis Barber/PhotoEdit; (b) C. C. Lockwood/DRK Photo. C35: John Serafin. C36: (bg) Grant Heilman/Grant Heilman Photography. C37: Ken Karp. C38: (bl) Charles Mauzy/Natural Selection; (br) Emma Lee/Life File/Photodisc. C39: (t) David R. Frazier/Photo Researchers, Inc.; (b) John Elk III. C40: (t) Don and Pat Valenti/DRK Photo; (b) Gary Gray/DRK Photo. C41: (i) Will and Deni McIntyre/Photo Researchers, Inc.; (t) American Museum of Natural History; (b) George Gerster/Photo Researchers, Inc. C42: (t) Ruth Dixon/Stock • Boston; (b) David Ulmer/Stock • Boston. C43: (l) Simon Fraser/Science Photo Library/Photo Researchers, Inc.; (r) Ken Karp. C44: (tl) Larry Lefever/Grant Heilman Photography; (tml) Eye Wire; (tm) R.J. Erwin/DRK Photo; (bl) Tony Freeman/PhotoEdit; (br) Hutchings Photography. C45: (l) Michael P. Gadomski/Photo Researchers, Inc. C46: (t) David Young-Wolfe/PhotoEdit; (b) Chromosohm/Sohm/Stock • Boston. C47: (t) Bonnie Kaman/PhotoEdit; (t) Spencer Grant/PhotoEdit. C50: Addison Geary/Stock • Boston. C52: (bg) Allen Prier/Panoramic Images. C53: (t) Peter Miller/Panoramic Images; (tm) Richard Sisk/Panoramic Images; (m) Mark Heifner/Panoramic Images; (bm) Kim Heacox/Tony Stone Images; (bl) Jack Krawczak/Panoramic Images; (br) Don Pitcher/Stock • Boston. C56: (tl) Jim Wiebe/Panoramic Images; (tr) Peter Pearson/Tony Stone Images; (bm) Mark Heifner/Panoramic Images; (bl) Richard Sisk/Panoramic Images; (br) Tom Bean/Tony Stone Images. C57: Jack Krawczak/Panoramic Images. C58: (bg) David L. Brown/Panoramic Images. C59: Ken Karp. C60: (t) Michael P. Gadomski/Photo Researchers, Inc.; (b) John Anderson/Earth Scenes. C61: Ken Karp. C62: (i) Photodisc; (t) Thomas Fletcher/Stock • Boston; (b) Jeff Greenberg/PhotoEdit. C63: (t) Kathy Ferguson/PhotoEdit; (b) Runk/Schoenberger/Grant Heilman Photography. C64: Ken Karp. C65: PhotoEdit. C66: (bg) The National Archives/Corbis; (i) Adam

Jones/Photo Researchers, Inc.; (t) W. E. Ruth/Bruce Coleman Inc. C67: (i) Pat Armstrong/Visuals Unlimited; (m) Sylvan H. Wittaver/Visuals Unlimited; (b) John Sohlden/Visuals Unlimited. C68: (bg) David Young-Wolfe/PhotoEdit. C69: Ken Karp. C70: (t) Ana Laura Gonzalez/Earth Scenes; (b) Art Montes De Oca/FPG International. C72: (t) David Bartruff/FPG International; (b) Will & Deni McIntyre/Photo Researchers, Inc. C73: G. Brad Lewis/Tony Stone Images. C74: (t) David Weintraub/Stock • Boston; (b) Archive photos/Library of Congress. C78: (bg) Fred Bavendam/Peter Arnold Inc.; (t) Dawn Wright/Dawn Wright; (b) Peter Ryan/Scripps Science Photo Library/Photo Researchers, Inc. C79: Mark M. Lawrence/The Stock Market.

National Geographic Unit Opener D: D00: Earth Satellite Corporation/Science Photo Library/Photo Researchers, Inc. D0 John Sanford/Science Photo Library/Photo Researchers, Inc D1: Science Photo Library/Photo Researchers, Inc; Photo Library Int'l/Photo Researchers, Inc. **Unit D:** D2: Jack Krawczyk/Panoramic Images. D4: (bg) Ariel Skelley/The Stock Market. D5: Ken Karp. D6: Ken Karp. D9: (l) Didier Givois/Photo Researchers, Inc.; (r) Ken Karp. D10: David Young-Wolfe/PhotoEdit. D11: Barbara Stotzen/PhotoEdit. D12: Paul & LindaMarie Ambrose/FPG International. D13: Howard Bluestein/Photo Researchers, Inc. D14: (bg) Clifford Paine/Corbis. D15: Ken Karp. D16: (t) Myrleen Ferguson/PhotoEdit; (m) Paul Silverman/Paul Silverman; (b) Michael Newman/PhotoEdit. D17: (t) Diane Hirsch/Fundamental Photographs; (b) Jeff Greenberg/Peter Arnold Inc. D20: Ken Karp. D21: P. Quittemelle/Stock • Boston. D22: (bg) Bob Krist/Corbis. D23: Dave Mager. D24: (tr) Tom Pantages; (l) Tom Pantages; (br) Jeff J. Daly/Stock • Boston. D25: (t) Charles D. Winters/Photo Researchers, Inc.; (br) Ken Karp; (bl) Tony Freeman/PhotoEdit. D27: (b) NOAA/Science photo Library/Photo Researchers, Inc. D28: (t) Michael P. Gadomski/Photo Researchers, Inc.; (b) Michael P. Gadomski/Photo Researchers, Inc. D29: F. Stuart Westmorland/Photo Researchers, Inc. D32: Michael Hovell/Index Stock Imagery. D34: (bg) Robert Mathena/Fundamental Photographs. D35: Ken Karp. D37: (t) Ken Lucas/Visuals Unlimited; (b) Thomas Barbudo/Panoramic Images. D40: Ken Karp. D41: Bob Daemmrich/Stock • Boston. D42: Jim Ballard/All Stock/PNI; David Nunuk/Science Photo Library/Photo Researchers, Inc. D44: (bg) Peter Menzel/Stock • Boston. D45: Ken Karp. D46: John R. Foster/Photo Researchers, Inc. D47: John Sanford/Photo Researchers, Inc. D48: NASA/Science Source/Photo Researchers, Inc. D49: (l) Mark E. Gibson/Visuals Unlimited; (r) NASA/Science Photo Library/Photo Researchers, Inc. D52: (bg) Frank Zullo/Photo Researchers, Inc. D53: Ken Karp. D56: (t) U.S .Geological Survey/Photo Researchers, Inc; (m) NASA/Mark Marten/Photo Researchers, Inc.; (bl) Stock • Boston; (br) NASA/Tom Pantages. D57: (tl) Ross Ressmeyer/NASA/Corbis; (tr) NASA/Photo Researchers, Inc.; (ml) Space Telescope Space Institute/Photo Researchers, Inc.; (mr) NASA/Tom Pantages. D57: (b) Space Telescope Space Institute/Photo Researchers, Inc. D58: (t) Tony Freeman/PhotoEdit; (b) Ken Karp. D62: (bg) Pekka Parvaiainen/Science Photo Library/Photo Researchers, Inc.; (i) Seth Shostak/Seth Shostak. D63: Seth Shostak/Seth Shostak. D64: Ken Karp.

National Geographic Unit Opener E: E0: James Marshall/The Stock Market. E1: Ron Stroud/Masterfile. **Unit E:** E2: Bernard Asset/Photo Researchers, Inc. E4: (bg) S. Dalton/DRK Photo, Researchers, Inc. E5: (t) Will Hart/PhotoEdit; (b) Ken Karp. E6: (tl) Gregory K. Scott/Photo Researchers, Inc.; (tr) Foodpix; (ml) Gregory K. Scott/Photo Researchers, Inc.; (mr) Foodpix; (bl) Zoran Milich/Allsport USA; (br) Zoran Milich/Allsport USA. E7: (t) Ken Karp; (b) Ken Karp. E8: (bg) The Stock Market; (t) Robert Winslow; (b) Fritz Polking/Peter Arnold Inc. E9: (t) Joseph Van Os/Image Bank; (b) Peter Weimann/Animals Animals. E12: (bg) Craig J. Brown/Flashfocus. E16: (l) NASA; (r) Hutchings Photography. E17: NASA/Earth Scenes. E18: Photodisc. E19: (t) Art Resource. E20: Ken Karp. E23: (i) Ken Karp. E26: (i) Tony Freeman/PhotoEdit; (b) John Coletti/Stock • Boston. E27: Bob Daemmrich/Stock • Boston. E28: (r) Ken Karp. E30: (bg) Hulton Getty; (l) Michael Conroy/AP World Wide Photos. E31: (t) UPI/Corbis/Bettman; (b) Courtesy of Speedo. E34: Addison Geary/Stock • Boston. E38: (tl) David Young-Wolfe/PhotoEdit; (tr) Hutchings Photography; (bl) Hutchings Photography; (br) John Eastcott/YvaMomatiuk/DRK Photo. E39: (r) Ken Karp; David Matherly/Visuals Unlimited. E42: (bg) Bob Daennrich/Stock • Boston. E43: Ken Karp. E45: Ken Karp. E46: (m) Michael Newman/PhotoEdit; (m) Tony Freeman/PhotoEdit; (b) Siede Preis/Photodisc. E47: (t) Roger Wilmshurst; Frank Lane Picture Agency/Corbis; (m) Corbis; (b) Eric Roth/Flashfocus. E48: Ken Karp. E49: (t) Domenicho Fetti/The Granger Collection. E50: (l) Joan Iaconetti/Bruce Coleman Inc.; (r) David Mager. E51: David Mager. E52: (bg) McCutchean/Visuals Unlimited. E54: Richard Hutchings/Photo Researchers, Inc. E55: Donald Specker/Earth Scenes. E56: Mark Burnett/Stock • Boston. E57: (t) Photodisc; (m) Photodisc; (b) David Young-Wolfe/PhotoEdit. E59: Jodi Jacobson. E62: (bg) NASA/The Image Works; (i) Joe Skipper/Archive Photos/Reuters. E63: NASA. E64: (t) Ken Karp; (b) John Neubauer/PhotoEdit.